GLOBAL ECONOMIC STUDIES

IMPACT OF GLOBAL ECONOMIC CRISIS ON AGRICULTURE

GLOBAL ECONOMIC STUDIES

Additional books in this series can be found on Nova's website under the Series tab.

Additional E-books in this series can be found on Nova's website under the E-book tab.

AGRICULTURE ISSUES AND POLICIES

Additional books in this series can be found on Nova's website under the Series tab.

Additional E-books in this series can be found on Nova's website under the E-book tab.

GLOBAL ECONOMIC STUDIES

IMPACT OF GLOBAL ECONOMIC CRISIS ON AGRICULTURE

AUSTEN W. YOUNG
EDITOR

Nova Science Publishers, Inc.
New York

For permission to use material from this book please contact us:
Telephone 631-231-7269; Fax 631-231-8175
Web Site: http://www.novapublishers.com

LIBRARY OF CONGRESS CATALOGING-IN-PUBLICATION DATA

Impact of global economic crisis on agriculture / editor: Austen W. Young.
p. cm.
Includes index.
ISBN 978-1-61761-180-3 (softcover)
1. Global Financial Crisis, 2008-2009. 2. Agriculture--Economic aspects--United States. I. Young, Austen W.
HB3722.I47 2010
338.10973--dc22
2010027284

Published by Nova Science Publishers, Inc. † New York

Contents

PREFACE

This book explores the world economic crisis that began in 2008, and which has had major consequences for U.S. agriculture. The weakening of global demand because of emerging recessions and declining economic growth results in reduced export demand and lower agricultural commodity prices, compared with those in 2008. These, in turn, reduce U.S. farm income and place downward pressure on farm real estate values. So far, the overall impact on U.S. agriculture is not as severe as on the broader U.S. economy because the record-high agricultural exports, prices, and farm income in 2007 and 2008 put U.S. farmers on solid financial ground.

The world economic crisis that began in 2008 has major consequences for U.S. agriculture. The weakening of global demand because of emerging recessions and declining economic growth result in reduced export demand and lower agricultural commodity prices, compared with those in 2008. These, in turn, reduce U.S. farm income and place downward pressure on farm real estate values. So far, the overall impact on U.S. agriculture is not as severe as on the broader U.S. economy because the record-high agricultural exports, prices, and farm income in 2007 and 2008 put U.S. farmers on solid financial ground. Moreover, the debt equity ratios in agriculture tend to be more conservative than those in most other sectors of the economy. There is much uncertainty concerning the depth and extent of the crisis. The outcomes for U.S. agriculture depend on whether or not there is a global realignment of exchange rates to correct current macroeconomic imbalances.

In: Impact of Global Economic Crisis...
Editor: Austen W. Young

ISBN: 978-1-61761-180-3

Chapter 1

What the 2008/2009 World Economic Crisis Means for Global Agricultural Trade

May Peters, Mathew Shane and David Torgerson

Abstract

The global economic crisis that started in late 2008 has led to a sharp curtailment of international trade, including a short-term decline in the value of global agricultural trade of around 20 percent. While not uniform across commodities and regions, the trade impact appears to be stronger on crops than on livestock. Global agricultural trade after slowing will continue to grow in the future. Economic growth prospects of emerging and developing countries will be important in determining composition of trade toward increased high-value products. The crisis is leading to a realignment of exchange rates, and the ultimate resolution of the crisis will depend on adjustments in the exchange value of the U.S. dollar. The U.S. agricultural sector would benefit from a depreciating dollar, which results in high export earnings, high agricultural commodity prices, increased production, and increased farm income.

Keywords: World economic crisis, international agricultural markets, international agricultural trade, agricultural imports, agricultural exports, world economic growth

ACKNOWLEDGMENTS

The authors would like to acknowledge the support and assistance of Janet Perry of USDA's Economic Research Service (ERS), who helped coordinate the production of the report. We appreciate the input from Shahla Shapouri and Stacey Rosen (food security) and would like to thank all of the reviewers for their helpful comments and suggestions, including David Orden, International Food Policy Research Institute; Munisamy Gopinath, Oregon State University; Shiva Makki, World Bank; Keith Weibe, United Nations Food and Agriculture Organization; David Stallings, USDA, Office of the Chief Economist; and William Liefert, Suchada Langley, Cheryl Christensen, and Sally Thompson, ERS. We also appreciate the editorial and design assistance of Priscilla Smith and Susan DeGeorge.

ECONOMIC CRISIS WILL TRANSFORM GLOBAL FINANCIAL SYSTEM

The ongoing global economic crisis that started in the United States in late 2008 and quickly spread to Europe and other economies around the world will have a far-reaching impact, particularly in the short term. Not only is the global financial system being transformed by it, but a worldwide, likely permanent restructuring of the international economy is occurring. In the short term, with negative growth in world gross domestic product (GDP), trade will decline and agriculture as a heavily trade-dependent sector will have to adjust accordingly. While the timeframe and severity of the global crisis is still largely unknown, some of its possible effects can be inferred for sectors such as agriculture, using projections based on likely alternative macroeconomic outcomes.

The volume of global trade in 2009 will decline for the first time since 1982 (World Bank, 2009). The International Monetary Fund (IMF) projects that the volume of goods imported by developed countries will decline by 3.1 percent this year and the emerging and developing countries will experience an unprecedented 1-percent decline in the volume of their exports. These projections appear to be conservative, as current information indicates that the decline in the value of merchandise trade in the first quarter of 2009 is 20 percent or more (see box, "Global Merchandise and Agricultural Trade Are Declining in the Short Run"). The value of China's exports in the first quarter of 2009 declined on a year-to-year basis by 20 percent, and the value of U.S. exports also fell during the first 2 months of 2009 by 22 percent, compared with 2008 exports' value. The value of merchandise imports of the European Union (EU), South Korea, Mexico, and the United States declined by 30 percent during the first several months of 2009 in comparison to the previous year. The discrepancy between the IMF estimate of the percentage decline in trade and the reported declines in value of trade indicate that a substantial part of the decline in value is due to falling prices. This suggests that consumption is not falling as sharply as the decline in the value of trade. Preliminary results show that there will be short-term declines in agricultural trade. This decline will result in lower agricultural prices and reduced farm incomes around the world.

The worsening of global economic conditions is also creating the potential for much more serious food-security challenges in traditionally food-insecure developing countries, as well as in some countries that have not experienced major food insecurity in recent years (Shapouri et al., 2009). Declines in export earnings for some countries as well as fewer remittances returning to those countries' economies from their citizens working abroad are eroding purchasing power while food prices, despite declining agricultural commodity prices, remain higher than they were before the 2008 price spike.

The global financial crisis and recession will affect each country differently depending on the country's linkages to the world economy, its economic condition before the crisis, and the degree to which it participates in the global financial markets. For example, China and India are likely to emerge from this crisis in relatively strong economic positions in contrast to developed countries such as the European Union, partly because they started out with very strong economic growth prior to the recession. In addition, the way in which the macroeconomic imbalances that contributed to the crisis are resolved will affect the realignment of exchange rates and economic growth prospects worldwide. The impact of that resolution and realignment is being felt in new trade patterns in 2009. While Canada and Mexico have continued to be the largest two markets for U.S. agricultural exports over the past few years, by the end of 2008 and into 2009, China had become the third most important destination for U.S. agricultural exports (USDA, FATUS, 2009).

Global Merchandise and Agricultural Trade Are Declining in the Short Run

The latest data on the value of total and agricultural merchandise trade show a broad-based decline in the value of exports and imports compared with a year ago (World Trade Atlas, 2009). The data also show that the decline in merchandise trade has accelerated considerably during the first quarter of 2009. This is consistent with a deepening of the economic recession worldwide.

Global agricultural trade shows decline in the short run

		Agricultural trade value		Value of total merchandise trade	
Country/ region	Latest month of available data	Fourth quarter (Oct-Dec) 2007-2008	First quarter (Jan-March) 2008-2009	Fourth quarter (Oct-Dec) 2007-2008	First quarter (Jan-March) 2008-2009
Percent change (value of exports)[1]					
China	March 2009	-0.4	-17.3	4.0	-19.7
Japan	March 2009	-15.6	-53.7	-9.8	-38.6
United States	February 2009	-5.5	-24.3	-4.0	-22.5
European Union	January 2009	-10.0	-33.7	-11.4	-33.2
Percent change (value of imports)[1]					
South Korea	March 2009	-3.3	-32.0	-9.0	-32.9
Mexico	January 2009	-2.7	-26.4	-6.1	-30.0
United States	February 2009	6.1	-11.7	-9.2	-30.4
European Union	January 2009	-11.8	-31.9	-10.6	-30.3

[1] Represents year-over-year percentage change.
Source: World Trade Atlas, 2009.

Total and agricultural merchandise trade should recover when the recession ends and economies begin to grow again. Many forecasts indicate that this is not likely to occur until the last quarter of 2009 or 9 case, then the decline in value of agricultural trade in the last quarter of 2008

How Shocks to the Global Economy Affect Agriculture

The economic crisis will affect international agriculture trade primarily through the realignment of real (adjusted for inflation) exchange rates and that realignment's effect on real incomes. The economic crisis has resulted in major recessions[1] in most of the major countries of the world, with world GDP expected to decline in 2009 by more than 2 percent (table 1). The slowing of the growth in demand for agricultural commodities worldwide— resulting from the fall in global income—has led to a slowing of the growth in the volume of agricultural commodities traded.

In addition, the large global imbalances in financial and merchandise trade that existed before the crisis likely will lead to substantial changes in exchange rates. Already the current crisis has led to the appreciation of the U.S. dollar against the currencies of those countries most affected by the crisis as investors seeking safe returns increased their purchases of U.S. Treasury bonds. This movement of funds led to a 15-percent appreciation of the dollar relative to its major trading partners between July 2008 and March 2009 (USDA, ERS Agricultural Exchange Rate Data Set, 2009). The appreciation of the U.S. dollar creates a competitive advantage in global markets for other major agricultural exporters, such as the EU, Australia, Canada, and Brazil. As U.S. products become relatively higher priced when the U.S. dollar increases in value, world demand increases for imports from countries whose currencies have declined in value relative to the U.S. dollar.

In addition to the impact on agriculture from these exchange-rate shifts, there are also the implications for agriculture of the effect of the crisis on energy prices and demand (figure 1). With the decline in GDP around the world and dramatically lower crude oil prices, profitability and prices of biofuels (ethanol and biodiesel) have decreased. Declining prices are not all bad, however, and the lower input and animal feed costs implied by the reduced energy prices will be beneficial to agricultural producers.

Changes in GDP and real exchange rates are emphasized in this analysis because of their importance in determining agricultural trade (Shane et al., 2008). Changes in the macroeconomy affect trade mainly through its impact on income and relative prices. GDP determines the amount a country has to spend while exchange rates determine how much it costs to exchange exported goods for imported ones. Both have major impacts on the quantity of goods produced and consumed and on trade patterns. A similar approach emphasizing the importance of income and relative prices on trade was used in analysis of impacts of past financial crisis on U.S. and international agriculture (Shane and Stallings, 1987). The other major determinants of trade—differences in production technology, factor endowments, and productivity—are implicit in the analysis while other macroeconomic variables—inflation, savings, investments, and interest rates—are accounted for in our macroeconomic model.

Table 1. The global recession is broad-base

• United States	• Hungary
• Canada	• Turkey
• Mexico	• Iran
• Argentina	• Japan
• Brazil	• Korea
• Chile	• Taiwan
• Colombia	• Hong Kong
• Costa Rica	• Singapore
• European Union	• Malaysia
• Norway	• Thailand
• Switzerland	• Australia
• Baltic States	• New Zealand
• Russia	• South Africa
• Ukraine	

Note: This is a partial list of countries with negative projected annual economic growth rate as of July 2009. Relatively small economies were not included in the list. Source: Global Insight, 2009.

The potential effects of the resolution of the economic crisis on international trade are important for U.S. agriculture. Highly dependent on world agricultural trade, the United States is a major participant in global markets for grains, oilseeds, cotton, and meat. A long-term reduction in worldwide import demand for agricultural commodities is likely to lead to a reduction in U.S. agricultural exports and to constrain U.S. farm income and agricultural commodity prices for some time to come.

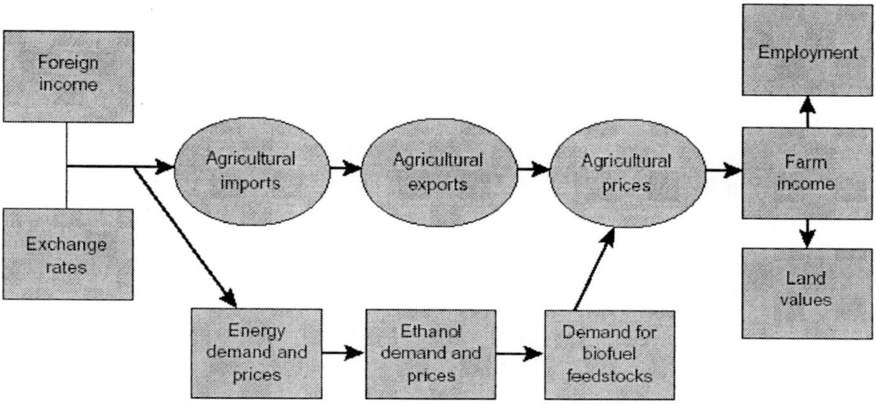

Source: ERS analysis.

Figure 1. Foreign macroeconomic linkages to agriculture

These effects were already evident in the early results from 2009. The declines in incomes around the world as a result of the evolving global recession combined with the short-term appreciation of the U.S. dollar is likely to result in significant declines in U.S. agricultural exports and lower agricultural prices, farm income, and employment in the American farm sector. But, because U.S. agriculture came into the crisis following record-high prices and income, and because U.S. farm balance sheets contain a much smaller percentage of debt than most other businesses, the impact of the crisis will likely be less on U.S. agriculture than on other sectors of the economy (Shane et al., 2009). However, in 2009 and perhaps 2010, U.S. agricultural producers are expected to operate in a less favorable economic environment and experience a decline in farm income before most macroeconomic factors start to return to historic trend levels. Agricultural households also might suffer from declining income from off-farm jobs, as the economic recession in the United States ripples though to rural-based businesses.

More important perhaps than the immediate effects of the economic crisis on world agricultural markets is the effect the economic crisis will have on trade and world consumption in the longer term. As we have already seen, exchange rates and changes in economic growth and income can have a major impact on total agricultural commodity and merchandise trade. Consequently, how exchange rates and economic growth evolve as the world economy recovers also will have a major impact on the volume of international agricultural commodity trade and the outlook for agriculture in major trading countries, such as the United States.

There is much uncertainty about how the macroeconomic imbalances that existed before the crisis will be resolved and the impact the resolution of these imbalances will have on exchange rates and on economic growth prospects. This uncertainty focuses in large part on whether China and other developing countries will continue to run large trade surpluses with the United States and other developed countries. Those importers' decision on whether or not to maintain surpluses will determine the economic growth prospects for the United States and other countries and whether the realignment of exchange rates will lead to a depreciation of the U.S. dollar or not (see box, "Global Trade and Financial Imbalances Contribute to the Economic Crisis").

Even though the manner in which the macroeconomic imbalances will be resolved is unknown, the likely impact of the worldwide economic slowdown can be explored for agriculture using projections based on the existing macroeconomic conditions as of December 2008 and assumptions about the likely ways that the imbalances will be resolved. To do this, we developed three sets of assumptions about how the financial and merchandise trade imbalances will be resolved. Using those three scenarios, we analyze the potential impacts on economic growth, the realignment of exchange rates, global agricultural markets, and international trade.

Global Trade and Financial Imbalances Contribute to the Economic Crisis

The global macroeconomic imbalances that preceded the ongoing economic crisis can be summarized by describing what happened between two groups of countries. On one side are the "savers" (trade-surplus countries). China is a good example. On the other side are the "consumers," (trade-deficit countries) such as the United States.

In general, the saver countries maintained large trade surpluses by, among other things, maintaining an undervalued exchange rate. This resulted in large trade deficits in the consumer countries. These trade imbalances also were accompanied by savings and consumption imbalances between the two groups. These large global trade and macroeconomic imbalances led to large capital flows from the trade-surplus countries to the trade-deficit countries, resulting in a large stock of loanable funds in recipient countries. The increased liquidity in the banking systems and weak regulatory environment led to a large pool of risky loans and investments. Once interest rates began to rise and housing values began to fall in late 2007, the number of bad loans and loan defaults began to rise rapidly. All of these were the consequence of the unsustainable global imbalances, the outcome of which is the financial crisis.

The financial crisis, along with the bursting of the real-estate bubble in developed countries and high energy prices, reduced consumption and investment, which eventually lead to a full blown recession spreading across countries.

Source: ERS analysis.

Unsustainable global imbalances contribute to financial crisis

Adjustments to reduce or eliminate the imbalances will occur. If the adjustments that take place lead to an appreciation of the U.S. dollar, then the global economy will follow a path that will lead to continued unsustainable global imbalances. However, if the adjustments that take place lead to a depreciation of the dollar, the resulting reduction or elimination of global trade and fi nancial imbalances will put the world on a more sustainable growth path. A sustainable growth path is characterized by the highest possible rate of economic growth that does not generate resource inflation, a situation where resource demand does not outstrip resource supplies. This more balanced economy can persist until, eventually (although not inevitably), another unsustainable global imbalance develops and leads to another crisis, thus, another cycle.

SCENARIOS CREATE DIFFERENT ECONOMIC FUTURES

The reference scenario was developed to reflect the onset of the economic crisis and the likely adjustments that will take place in the economic growth and relative prices (exchange rates) in response to assumed changes in the macroeconomic imbalances due to the crisis. The front end of the reference scenario is the 2008 USDA long-term projections modified by replacing its exogenous macroeconomic information with Oxford global macroeconomic results based on December 2008 assumptions and the simulated impact of these changes in macroeconomic variables on world crop and livestock commodity supply and use (USDA, 2008).

The two alternative scenarios characterize two possible movements of real exchange rates, real economic growth rates, and other macroeconomic variables corresponding to how the global imbalances are resolved. The first considers a continuation of major trade and savings imbalances, assuming that they lead to a sustained movement toward appreciation of the U.S. dollar, while the second assumes a significant reduction in trade and savings imbalances and a major depreciation of the U.S. dollar.

Reference scenario. The reference scenario is based on the Oxford Model's longrun forecast of the global economy as of December 2008 (Oxford Economics, 2008). It reflected a consensus view at the time that the world and U.S. economies will recover by late 2009.[2] This scenario assumes modest adjustment in U.S. domestic savings, a slow appreciation of the U.S. dollar—19 percent over 10 years—and modest growth in U.S. and world GDP. U.S. economic growth through 2017 (2.5 percent per annum) is projected slower than experienced during the previous 10 years (3 percent per annum). It also assumes that future economic growth in other economies of the world will be slightly higher, at 4 percent per annum, than was true over the last decade.

Since December 2008—when assumptions were formulated—until mid-year 2009, the near-term prospects for economic growth have deteriorated with U.S. GDP declining by 5.5 percent in the first quarter of 2009 and the value of the dollar increasing. Whatever these events portend about economic growth in the short term, they are not yet viewed as determining the long-term exchange rate pattern or long-term growth prospects of the United States and other countries. While the December 2008 Oxford forecast was less severe than may be currently indicated, it captured much of the pattern which appears to be evolving and the overall longer term pattern of adjustment will likely be within the range of alternatives considered in this paper.

High dollar scenario. The first alternative scenario (high dollar scenario) of the global macro economy lays out a case in which exchange rates and finan-cial and macroeconomic imbalances return to pre-crisis levels. This could occur if developing countries, including China, continue to run large trade surpluses with developed economies such as the United States and the former continue to invest their excess savings in the latter. If that pattern continues, it would keep interest rates low, stimulate U.S. capital formation and economic growth and bid up the value of the U.S. dollar. As a result, U.S. economic growth in 2017 would be higher than it was in the reference while economic growth in the other countries of the world would be lower. The accompanying appreciation of the U.S. dollar, up 40 percent from 2008-17 reference levels, will make the value of the dollar higher than any other time since 1990 and 20 percent higher than its last peak in 1991.

Low dollar scenario. The second alternative scenario (low dollar scenario) of the global macro economy sets out a case in which global trade and financial imbalances decline and economic growth is renewed at long-term sustainable rates. For the United States, this would mean a real slowdown in the inflow of developing country savings, giving rise to lower U.S. trade deficits, higher domestic savings, and relatively low real investment. This is accompanied by a depreciation of the U.S. dollar against major foreign currencies. These assumptions are consistent with slower economic growth relative to the reference scenario for both the United States and the rest of the countries of the world through much of the time path of the analysis. The weaker U.S. dollar would mean it would take less foreign currency to equal a dollar, making U.S. agricultural exports less expensive for the rest of the world.

The effect of these changes on a specific country will depend both on the magnitude of the changes in income and exchange rates they face and the responsiveness of their agricultural markets to them. Hence, the impact of these changes will vary by country and by commodity. In addition, some countries account for a large share of the international export market and their responses will affect world prices significantly. The populations in most developing countries account for a small share of international trade and are price takers, which means they do not affect world commodity prices. Those populations spend a high proportion of income on food, so changes in world agricultural commodity prices will significantly affect the food consumption of these developing economies. To account for these differing responses to changes in macroeconomic conditions, we utilize a dynamic global agricultural trade model called Dynamic PEATSim (see box, "PEATSim Model Calibrates Each Country's Agricultural Activities to USDA Long-Term Projections").

The Oxford Model (2008), a global macroeconomic model, was used to develop consistent projections of the different macroeconomic variables including GDP, exchange rates, consumer price indexes (CPIs), and petroleum prices for each scenario or adjustment path. The projections were created by making assumptions about adjustments in trade and savings imbalances and seeing the resulting impact on the macro economy and on the above variables. Some of the Oxford outcomes (economic growth, exchange rates, and inflation) were then introduced into the PEATSim model as exogenous variables to determine the potential impact of these outcomes on agricultural commodity prices, consumption, production, and trade in different countries and regions of the world.

Given the extent of the economic crisis and the size of the economies affected, it is not possible to isolate the changes in GDP from changes in exchange rates, inflation, and other macroeconomic variables. They are all linked to each other and determined simultaneously. These dynamic interactions among the macroeconomic variables were captured by the Oxford model. Consequently, the scenarios used in PEATSim do not arbitrarily allow one variable such as GDP to change, while all other variables remain constant, as this will not relate to any relevant path of adjustment of the macro economy. Thus, the agricultural PEATSim model adopted scenarios that reflect relevant paths of adjustments in the corresponding set of macroeconomic variables generated by the Oxford model.

PEATSim Model Calibrates Each Country's Agricultural Activities to USDA Long-Term Projections

Dynamic PEATSim is a partial-equilibrium, multi-commodity, multi-region global gross trade model of the agriculture sector. It uses supply-and-demand equations to capture the economic behavior of producers, consumers, and markets in a global framework. It includes variables for production, area, yields, consumption, exports, imports, stocks, world prices, and domestic producer prices.

Identities such as supply and utilization, consumption and related items (food, feed, fuel, crush, other) hold for all commodities and regions in the model. The model calibrates each country's agricultural activities to the USDA's long-term projections (USDA, 2008).

The model balances supply and demand, and consequently prices are determined at market clearing levels that permit global market equilibrium to be achieved. PEATSim includes 13 countries or regions: the United States, the European Union,[3] Japan, Canada, Mexico, Brazil, Argentina, China, India, Australia, New Zealand, South Korea, and the rest of the world (ROW). Agricultural commodities covered include grains, oilseeds, and livestock products. The model's innovative and flexible specification gives it the ability to analyze a variety of scenarios. The PEATSim model is written in the GAMS (General Algebraic Modeling System) programming language utilizing PATH, a Mixed Complementarity Problem (MCP) Solver/Algorithm developed by Dirkse and Ferris (1995).

MCP allows PEATSim to generate a model with different production and consumption regimes, as well as utilize functions with disconti-nuities. It also allows an endogenous determination of which regimes are dominant for given market conditions and the evaluation of the consequences of regime shifts. The PEATSim model generates annual changes over a time path, in this case 2009-17. For a more exhaustive discussion of the PEATSim model's structural framework, see Peters et al. (2009).

Reference Scenario: Major Impacts on Agriculture Will Occur in 2009-11

Under the reference scenario, the greatest impact of the economic crisis will likely be experienced in 2009-11. Global GDP declines by 2 percent in 2009. GDP growth rates between 2008 and 2009 decline across all countries and regions by 2-5 percentage points (table 2).

While many countries, including the United States, experience negative growth, China and India still maintain positive growth in real GDP in 2009. During the height of the crisis, in 2009, GDP declines in developed countries, but continues to increase for many emerging and developing countries. As shown in figure 2, income growth will rebound strongly in 2010 for most countries and continue to grow for several years through 2012. Economic growth will then begin to slow through 2014 before stabilizing around its new longrun trend through 2017. For most countries, income growth will start returning to near trend rates after 2011 as shown in figure 2.

Table 2. All countries experience income declines

Country/region	Percentage-point change in real GDP growth rates between 2008 and 2009
Argentina	-4.1
Australia	-2.1
Brazil	-3.8
Canada	-1.9
China	-2.1
European Union	-2.9
India	-2.5
Japan	-2.6
Mexico	-2.1
New Zealand	-3.1
South Korea	-4.7
United States	-3.2
Rest of the world (ROW)	-2.5
World (total)	-2.8

Note: GDP = Gross Domestic Product.

Source: Oxford Economics, December 2008.

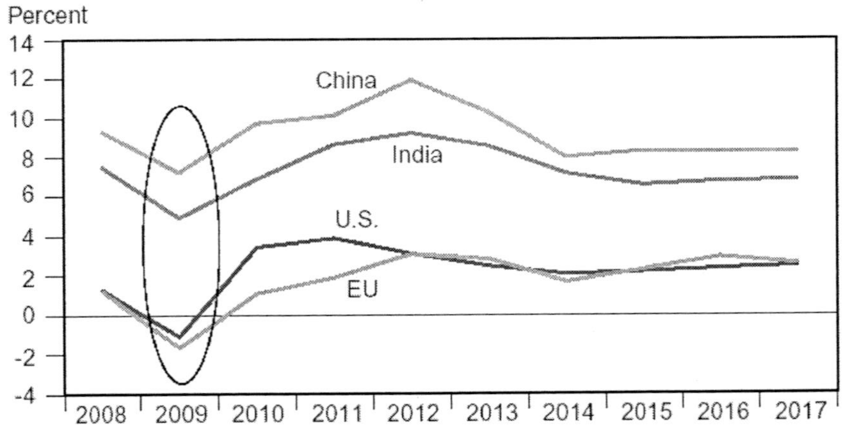

Source: Oxford Economics, December 2008.

Figure 2. Real GDP contracts in many countries in 2009

Agricultural Consumption Patterns Continue at a Reduced Rate

In the reference scenario, contraction in GDP growth in 2008 and 2009 does not lead to a contraction in consumption of most agricultural commodities. This is largely due to how the changes in GDP are distributed among the leading consuming countries. China, India, United States, and the EU-27 have been consistently among the top five consumers of many of the agricultural commodities (figure 3). Given their consumers' high levels of per capita income and inelastic food demand, reductions in GDP are not likely to cause food consumption to decline in the United States or European Union. Consumers in China and India will be more sensitive to changes in GDP because of their low levels of per capita income. While GDP growth in these countries will slow, it is still expected to grow by more than 5 percent in 2009. Trends in consumption in emerging and developing countries that existed before the crisis, such as the movement of diets toward increased meat consumption, will likely continue although at a slower rate.

The contraction in global GDP that occurs under the reference case does, however, lead to a significant slowing of growth in the consumption of agricultural commodities. Growth in world food crop and feed crop consumption begins slowing in 2009 as a result of the recession (table 3). World consumption of wheat and corn stagnates, up less than 0.5 percent above 2008 levels. Consumption of corn strengthens sharply in 2010, reflecting the upturn in GDP as the world economic situation improves. Wheat consumption strengthens somewhat in 2010, but growth remains below 1 percent. Beef and pork consumption remains fairly strong in 2009, growing by nearly 2 and 3 percent respectively. Beef and veal consumption moderates slightly in 2010, while growth in pork consumption slows by about 1 percentage point.

The decline in consumption growth is greater outside of the United States, reflecting international agricultural markets' greater sensitivity to the economic crisis relative to U.S. agricultural markets. Wheat consumption outside the United States slows in 2009, increasing only 0.3 percent above 2008 levels. Consumption strengthens slightly in 2010, but growth remains below 1 percent. Growth in consumption of corn outside the United States also slows substantially growing by 0.3 percent, but regains strength in 2010, increasing by nearly 2 percent.

Table 3. GDP Contraction Slows Consumption

Commodity	Country/ region	Quantity consumed, annual growth rates, reference scenario				
		2009	2010	2015	2016	2017
		Percent				
Food crops						
Rice	World	-0.4	1.0	1.0	0.8	1.0
	Less U.S.	-0.5	1.0	1.0	0.8	1.0
Wheat	World	0.4	0.8	1.2	0.8	1.3
	Less U.S.	0.3	0.7	1.2	0.8	1.4
Feed crops						
Corn	World	0.4	1.8	2.0	1.4	1.9
	Less U.S.	0.3	1.9	2.4	1.6	2.2
Other coarse						
grains	World	0.8	0.7	0.8	0.3	1.0
	Less U.S.	1.2	1.1	0.8	0.3	1.0
Livestock						
Beef and veal	World	1.7	1.5	2.2	1.1	2.9
	Less U.S.	2.5	2.1	2.3	1.2	3.4
Pork	World	2.7	1.5	2.4	1.8	2.7
	Less U.S.	2.8	1.9	2.6	1.9	2.9

Source: PEATSim results.

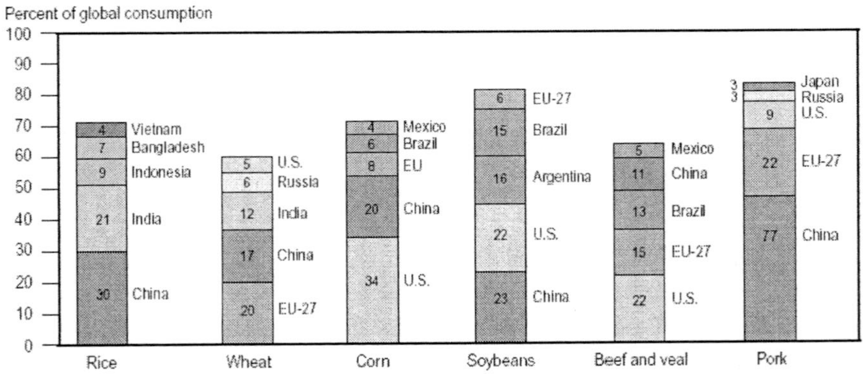

Source: USDA's Foreign Agricultural Trade of the United States (FATUS) database, 2009.

Figure 3. China, India, United States, and EU-27 led global consumption in 2008

Growth in foreign consumption of beef and pork remains stronger than U.S. growth, reflecting the continued increase in incomes in major emerging markets, such as China, where consumer diets continue to diversify away from grains and toward consumption of more meat. Consumption of beef and pork in other economies around the world grows by 2.5 and 2.8 percent in 2009 before slowing modestly to around 2 percent in 2010.

By 2015-17, growth in consumption of most commodities recovers and stabilizes to pre-crisis levels. As a result, growth in agricultural trade will likely strengthen over this time frame as well. Based on these results, it does not appear that the economic crisis will alter the ongoing changes in diet and food consumption in developing and emerging countries. Consumption of feed for animals and of meat outside the United States grow faster than consumption of food grains as slower, but positive growth in GDP continues in emerging and developing countries. However, a steeper decline in economic growth over a longer period could lead to a reversal of the change toward meat consumption, particularly if growth in GDP in emerging and developing countries turns negative.

World Agricultural Prices Decline While Agricultural Production Slows

The lower rate of consumption growth translates into decreased demand for agricultural commodities, which also affects commodity prices.

World prices (in real terms) of crops and livestock products decline rapidly from their peak in 2008, with most of the decline occurring in the end of 2008 and the beginning of 2009. The sharp decline is a result of the slowing of consumption growth due to the rapid increase in agriculture commodity prices from 2004-08, an increase in supply in response to the high prices, and the appreciation of the U.S. dollar. World and domestic producer prices stabilize around their trend starting in 2012 and remain stable through the remainder of the time period in the reference scenario.

The decline in producer prices from their peak 2007-08 levels leads to slowing of production. In general, production of most of the selected food crops, feed crops, and livestock products in the reference scenario slows or declines from 2009-10 and then begins to strengthen by 2011 as the economy recovers (table 4). For example, the production of wheat outside the United

States slows sharply from a 5.9-percent increase in 2008 to a 1.2-percent increase in 2009.

Production continues to slow in 2010, turning negative as a time lag occurs for producers responding to the decline in real prices. Wheat production increases slightly in 2011. Growth in foreign production of feed crops, as reflected by corn, slows from 2.7 percent in 2009 to 1.9 percent in 2010 before increasing by 2.1 percent in 2011. Despite this decline in growth, feed crop production remains stronger than production of food crops, such as wheat, whose growth stagnates through 2011, down -0.1 percent in 2010 and up 0.2 percent in 2011.

The effect of lower prices on meat production does not become evident in this scenario until 2010, reflecting in part the time it takes for increases in feed costs to affect production decisions. Growth in beef production continues to contract in 2011, reflecting the length of time it takes to make adjustments in herd size in response to lower prices.

Growth in foreign production of meat, such as beef and veal, slows through 2011 as well, but at 1.4 percent, also grows faster than food grains production. The relative strength of growth in production of feed grains and meat reflects the continued shifting of diets to meat in emerging and developing countries even as global consumption growth slows.

Production changes for specific commodities in individual countries will depend on the relative changes in exchange rates, domestic policies, and economic conditions of a country or region. The top five producers worldwide of selected crops and livestock products accounted for 70 to 90 percent of global production in 2008 (figure 4).

Table 4. Production Slows with Slackening of Demand, but Strengthens in 2011

Commodity	Country/region	2009	2010	2011
		Percentage change in production		
Food crop Wheat	World less U.S.	1.2	-0.1	0.2
Feed crop Corn	World less U.S.	2.7	1.9	2.1
Livestock Beef and veal	World less U.S.	2.9	1.8	1.4

Source: PEATSim results.

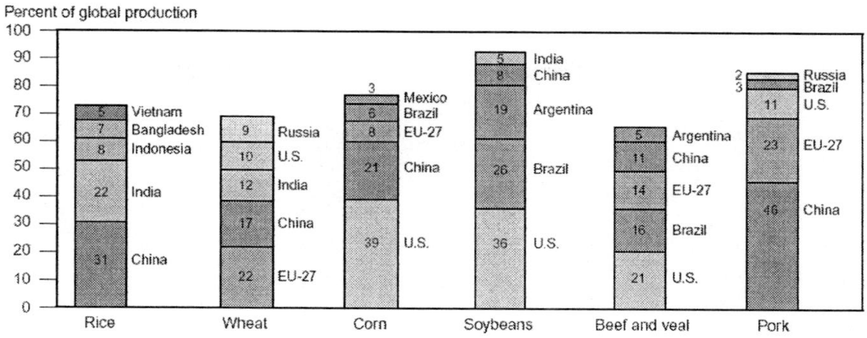

Source: USDA's Foreign Agricultural Trade of the United States (FATUS) database, 2009.

Figure 4. China, EU-27, United States, and Brazil were top global crop and meat producers in 2008

China, India, EU, United States, Brazil, and Argentina rank near the top of the list for each of the different commodities. Consequently any change in world production will be dominated by changes in production in these countries that result from farmers responding to changes in demand.

Global Agricultural Trade Slows

In addition to its impact on prices, the slowing of consumption also leads to a slowing of growth in trade of agricultural commodities from 2009-10. The slowing in growth in trade in the reference scenario will have the greatest effect on U.S. producers and its major competitors in world export markets. Figure 5 shows leading exporters and importers of selected agricultural commodities in 2008.

The United States is consistently one of the top exporters for all the agricultural commodities shown. Canada, Brazil, and EU are other major exporters. Japan, while not a major exporter, is a major importer of corn, other coarse grains, soybean seeds, soy meal, beef and pork. Mexico, a large trading partner of the United States, is a major importer of corn, and imports a considerable amount of the rest of the commodities as well. Canada, also a major U.S. trading partner, does not rank in the top five leading importers globally.

Some countries or regions that are major producers and consumers of agricultural crops and livestock do not play prominent or direct roles in international markets. However, domestic market conditions and events in these regions do affect global agricultural trade. For example, a major producer and consumer such as China may not be trading much in proportion to its total production and consumption for certain commodity, yet a significant decline in its domestic production or an increase in domestic consumption will raise China's import needs, putting pressure on the international market.

In addition, China historically has exported some commodities (e.g., rice, wheat, corn, other coarse grains, soybeans, soy meal, beef and veal, pork, and poultry) and continues to do so in the very beginning of the reference scenario's time path (2009-10). China, however, turns into a net importer of many agricultural commodities in later years of this scenario due to growing population and expected strong income growth. Thus, domestic conditions in large producing or consuming countries such as China can and will affect international markets.

Table 5 shows the growth rate of global quantity imported (same as global quantity exported) of selected agricultural commodities over the period 2009-11 under the reference scenario.

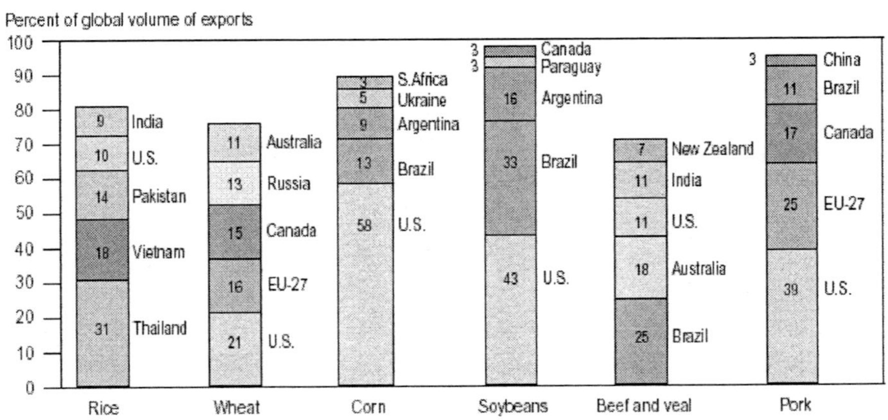

Source: USDA's Foreign Agricultural Trade of the United States (FATUS) database, 2009.

Figure 5. United States led exporters globally in 2008

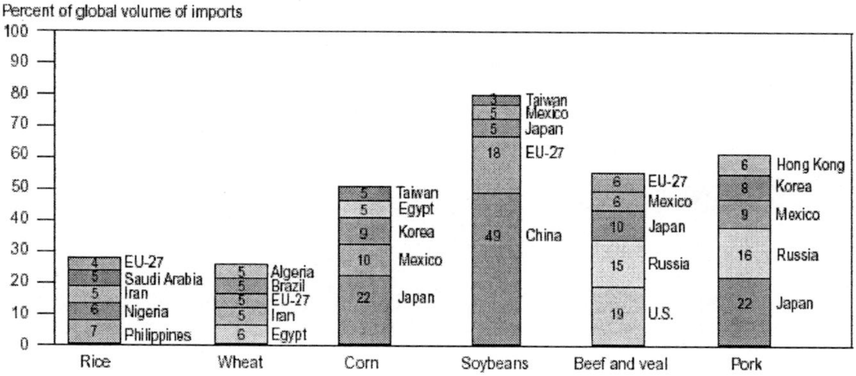

Source: USDA's Foreign Agricultural Trade of the United States (FATUS) database, 2009.

Figure 6. Major importers were generally not major producers of crops and meat, 2008

While the rate of growth in global imports slows through 2010 as a result of the slowing of consumption, it remains positive for most agriculture commodities as global imports continue to grow (table 5). The rate of growth in imports from 2009-11 remains positive for all commodities covered in this analysis, except for pork in 2009 and rice in 2010. As the economy recovers, by 2011 growth of global imports of all commodities, except poultry, starts to strengthen. Global import growth then remains strong for most commodities through 2017, with corn showing the weakest growth. The poor performance of corn possibly reflects the increasing diversion of corn for the production of ethanol in the United States during this period.

As with global imports, growth in the imports of countries outside the United States increases for all commodities, except pork in 2009 and rice in 2010. Growth in meat imports outside the United States generally slows in 2010, but remains positive, with beef and veal imports growing by 0.1 percent. Growth in foreign imports of feed crops slows in 2010 as well before gaining in strength in 2011. Foreign imports of corn slow to 2.4 percent in 2010 before increasing by 5.0 percent in 2011. Nonetheless foreign imports of feed crops generally grow faster than foreign food crop imports.

The continued strength in growth of foreign meat and feed crop imports are consistent with the consumption results. It is likely a result of the positive economic growth in emerging and developing countries which allows for the continued convergence of the composition of their diets toward the diets of developed countries and toward high-value products. The continued strength of foreign meat and feed crop imports also demonstrates that continued economic growth in the emerging and developing countries is a factor in the long-term increase in agriculture imports.

The strength of import growth outside the United States means some U.S. producers will be able to increase their exports during the economic crisis. Given the growth in foreign meat and feed crop imports, those commodities have potential for U.S. export growth.

Table 5. Growth in global agricultural import slows in 2009-10

Commodity	Country/region[1]	Growth rate in quantity traded, reference scenario		
		2009	2010	2011
		Percent		
Rice	World	7.2	-5.1	1.2
Wheat	World	5.6	1.2	4.5
Corn	World	5.7	2.4	5.0
Soybeans	World	4.4	3.3	5.4
Beef and veal	World	6.7	0.7	1.1
Pork	World	-3.6	1.3	3.4
Poultry	World	8.1	4.8	3.2

Source: PEATSim results.

[1] The United States is a minor importer, therefore world less U.S. growth rates will be very close to global growth rates.

Global exports of meat and food and feed grains mirror changes in global imports in our reference scenario. Global export growth slows but remains positive through 2010 before steadily increasing throughout the rest of the projection period (table 6). In addition, growth of global meat exports is generally greater than growth in global exports of food crops.

There is, however, the potential for significant changes in trade patterns due to the effect of appreciation of the U.S. dollar on the rate of growth in exports for the United States and other countries. In the short term (2009-11), when the greatest impact of the economic crisis is felt, foreign exports of most agricultural products grow faster than U.S. exports. During this period, growth in U.S. exports—which are relatively higher priced—generally lag behind its competitors as foreign exports grow faster.

In particular, foreign exports of corn, wheat, and soybeans generally grow faster than U.S. exports during this period. This is mainly due to the increased cost of U.S. products in foreign markets due to the modest appreciation of the dollar. In the reference scenario, the main beneficiaries of this reduction in U.S. competitiveness are the European Union and Australia for wheat, Argentina for corn, and Brazil for soybeans.

U.S. exports of meat generally increase faster than foreign meat exports during this period, particularly, with respect to poultry and beef and veal. These results reflect in part the strong growth in foreign meat imports during 2009-11 and the ability of U.S. meat producers to maintain their comparative advantage.

These trends with respect to U.S. crop and meat exports tend to hold over the long term as well. U.S. crop exports generally lag behind foreign crop exports, while U.S. meat exports generally continue to grow faster than foreign meat exports. Consequently, U.S. market share of global exports of wheat, corn, and soybeans all decline. The decline in U.S. export share for these products can be attributed to the steady appreciation of the U.S. dollar that occurs throughout this scenario as well. As in the case of corn, an increase in U.S. domestic use of corn for biofuel partly contributes to declines in exports as well. On the other hand, U.S. exports of poultry, pork, and beef and veal grow faster than foreign exports, enabling the United States to increase its market share of exports for these products.

Alternative Scenarios Rely on U.S. Dollar Appreciation or Depreciation

The two alternative scenarios (high dollar and low dollar) point to divergent paths for the resolution of financial and trade imbalances and the effect they will have on exchange rates and the value of the dollar (figure 7). The value of the dollar is determined using trade weighted exchange rates (ERS Exchange Rate Data Set, 2009). In the high dollar scenario, the value of the dollar continues to appreciate steeply against other currencies, eventually exceeding its 2005 value by over 30 percent. This would place the dollar higher than its previous peak, achieved in 1991. In the low dollar scenario, the value of the dollar returns to the path it was on before the economic crisis, steadily depreciating against major currencies through 2017. In this case, the depreciation of the value of the dollar bottoms out slightly below its value in 2008.

Table 6. Global export growth slows in 2009-10

Commodity	Country/region	Growth rate in quantity exported					
		2009	2010	2011	2015	2016	2017
		Percent					
Rice	World	7.2	-5.1	1.2	4.1	3.7	3.6
	World less U.S.	7.3	6.3	0.8	4.2	3.9	3.8
Wheat	World	5.6	1.2	4.5	4.1	2.3	2.9
	World less U.S.	7.8	0.1	6.1	5.1	2.9	3.5
Corn	World	5.7	2.4	5.0	1.7	0.8	1.5
	World less U.S.	8.7	1.0	15.3	-2.1	1.4	-2.4
Soybeans	World	4.4	3.3	5.4	3.4	1.6	3.1
	World less U.S.	16.3	2.2	8.2	4.2	2.3	3.9
Beef and veal	World	6.7	0.7	1.1	3.7	3.0	1.5
	World less U.S.	7.0	0.1	0.6	3.6	2.9	1.0
Pork	World	-3.6	1.3	6.4	3.3	3.7	3.7
	World less U.S.	8.3	-3.0	3.6	-0.8	2.2	-0.5
Poultry	World	8.1	4.8	3.2	2.1	4.5	2.7
	World less U.S.	26.4	2.8	2.0	-0.2	8.1	-0.3

Source: PEATSim results.

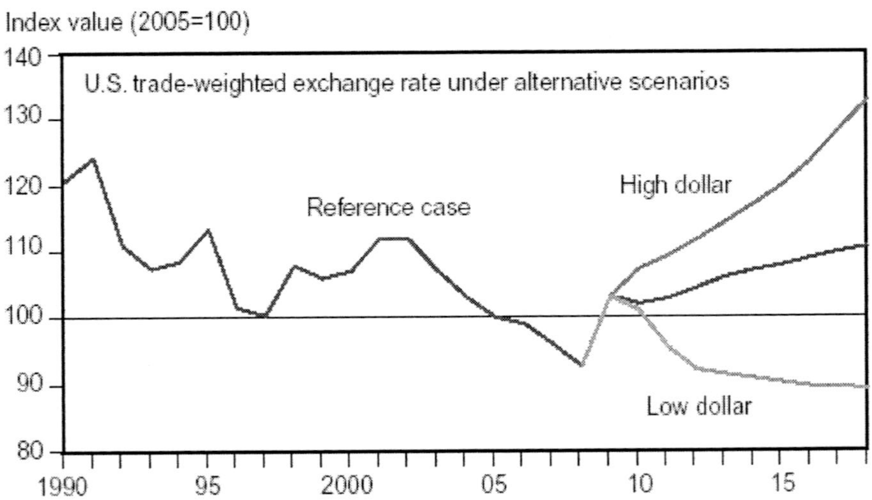

Source: USDA, ERS, International Macroeconomic Data Set and ERS estimates.

Figure 7. Future value of the U.S. dollar is uncertain

Whether or not exports of a specific commodity from a particular country/ region increase depends on the effects of the appreciation of the domestic currency against the U.S. dollar relative to the appreciation of other foreign currencies against the U.S. dollar and on effects of changes in domestic income on domestic supply and resulting demand conditions. In general, the depreciation of the U.S. dollar benefits U.S. agricultural producers because it reduces the cost of their products in world markets, allowing them to increase their exports. Consumers outside the United States also benefit because they face lower prices. On the other hand, the depreciation of the U.S. dollar is unfavorable to U.S. consumers because their dollars buy fewer products and to agricultural producers in the other economies because their goods become more costly relative to U.S. goods.

High Dollar Scenario: Foreign Markets Have Fewer Means to Buy More Expensive U.S. Goods

In the high dollar scenario, the U.S. recovery starts out weaker than in the reference case with U.S. real GDP in 2011 coming in about 2 percent lower (figure 8). U.S. GDP stays lower than the reference case through 2012. Starting in 2013, however, U.S. GDP moves permanently higher than the reference case (figure 8).

The opposite trend is seen in the other economies of the world. The recovery in the world (less United States) begins stronger than in the reference scenario continuing through 2013, at which point it trends below the reference GDP level through 2017. By 2011, Mexico and Brazil have GDP about 3 percent higher than the reference case (table 7).

The stronger GDP is primarily due to trade-induced exchange rate effects that cut trade deficits in other countries. Only Argentina experiences a 3-percent smaller GDP in 2011. In the transition year of 2013, GDP in Argentina and China is 3.0 and 1.5 percent weaker than in the reference case. Eventually all major countries start to have lower GDP than in the reference case. By the end of the high dollar scenario in 2017, only Australia and Korea have GDPs higher than in the reference scenario, about 2 and 4 percent higher respectively. Argentina's and Mexico's economies see GDP shrink the most from the reference case, with GDP coming in about 6 percent lower.

For the high dollar scenario, the slackening of economic growth and the increase in the value of the U.S. dollar relative to the reference scenario leads to a greater slowing of consumption relative to the reference case. This in turn leads to a decline in global demand. Thus, in the high dollar scenario, world agricultural prices (real terms), as expected, decline across all commodities throughout the time period.

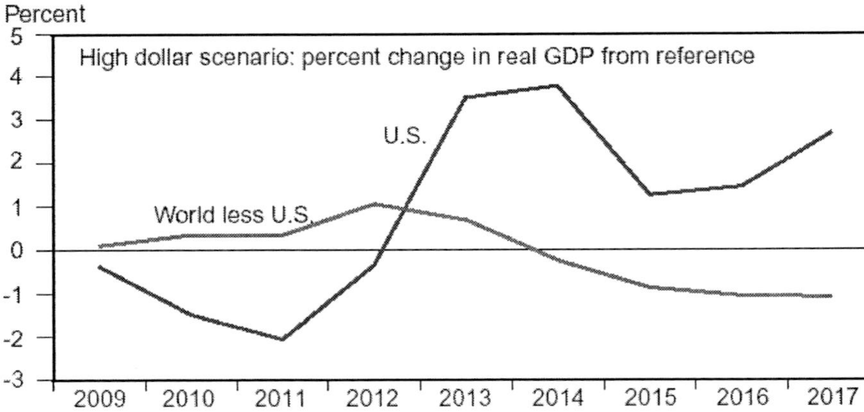

Source: Oxford Economics, December 2008.

Figure 8. U.S. real GDP increases relative to other economies of the world

Meanwhile, producer prices for agricultural commodities in the other countries/region of the world also decline. This reflects the decline in demand caused by reductions in income.

In the high dollar scenario, the weakened consumption growth in other countries of the world affects agricultural trade through lower GDP growth relative to the reference scenario over time. While starting out strong, the weakening of consumption over time in these countries causes world demand for agricultural imports to slow relative to the reference scenario.

Other country economies' imports of food and feed crops (table 8) track fairly closely the changes in GDP. Food and feed crop imports rise above the reference level through 2013. As GDP in these other economies starts to fall below the reference scenario, their imports of most food and feed crops start to drop below reference levels as well. By 2015, imports have declined 2 percent below reference levels for most food and grain crops, and remain below reference levels throughout the rest of the scenario. Reflecting greater sensitivity of meat consumption to the appreciation of the dollar, foreign imports of meat fall below reference levels from the onset and remain substantially below reference scenario levels through 2017.

Table 7. U.S. Real GDP Grows More When Dollar Appreciates

Country/region	Reference scenario			High dollar scenario			Low dollar scenario		
	2011	2013	2017	2011	2013	2017	2011	2013	2017
	GDP in $ billion (2000 dollars)			*Percent deviation from reference*			*Percent deviation from reference*		
United States	12,225	13,170	14,648	-2.1	3.5	2.7	1.8	-0.2	-1.8
European Union	9,887	10,420	11,423	0.0	0.3	0.0	-0.2	0.4	0.6
Japan	5,204	5,420	5,737	0.0	1.3	-0.9	-1.2	-0.3	0.9
Canada	932	995	1,127	0.5	0.0	-1.1	-0.5	-1.5	-4.8
Mexico	743	814	936	2.6	1.1	-6.4	-2.3	-6.5	-3.4
Brazil	926	1,008	1,160	3.5	4.7	-2.5	-3.7	-5.5	-7.1
Argentina	430	468	533	-2.6	-3.1	-5.9	-5.2	-8.8	-12.5
China	3,330	3,998	5,700	-0.4	-1.4	-3.3	0.0	2.8	-1.1
India	988	1,158	1,549	0.0	1.3	-2.3	-0.1	1.0	-1.6
Australia	538	577	663	1.0	1.4	2.3	0.5	0.7	0.2
New Zealand	69	74	82	0.5	-0.2	-0.5	0.3	0.2	0.4
South Korea	793	881	1,075	9.6	12.8	3.6	4.5	7.9	0.4
Rest of world	6,498	7,135	8,551	-0.2	0.0	-0.7	-0.2	0.0	-0.4

Source: Oxford Economics, December 2008; PEATSim results.

Effects for individual countries are mixed and depend on several factors, including relative changes in value of their own currencies against the U.S. dollar. Most countries though, experience declines in their imports from reference levels. The few countries with generally higher imports than the reference case include: EU for rice and beef; South Korea for corn; and United States for beef.

Exports of rice, wheat, and soybeans of the other countries of the world trend above their reference levels in the beginning of the time path, before falling below reference levels in 2015 and through the end of time path (table 8). The increase in their agricultural exports above reference levels through the first part of the time path reflects the rise in world (less United States) demand for agricultural imports during this period and the appreciation in the U.S. dollar. The latter development makes U.S. exports less competitive in international markets, allowing the other countries of the world to increase their market share. The effects of appreciation of the dollar and lower incomes relative to the reference scenario on global consumption eventually overwhelm the increase in their agricultural exports induced by changes in exchange rates. As a result, over the last few years of the time path, exports of these crops drop below their reference levels.

Trade in each individual country/region reacts uniquely to the assumptions for the scenarios. In the high dollar scenario, countries that have significantly higher agricultural exports than in the reference scenario in the initial years include: India for rice, Australia for wheat, Brazil for corn, Brazil and Argentina for soybeans, and EU for pork and poultry. These gains are temporary, however, as by the end of the time path (2017) exports fall below their reference levels for nearly all countries and commodities.

U.S. agricultural exports generally track lower than the reference levels for all commodities due to loss of market share resulting from the appreciation of the U.S. dollar. The departure from reference levels gets larger through time for most commodities due to the relatively lower GDP in countries outside the United States and the appreciation of the dollar. The lower aggregate demand reduces the foreign demand for agricultural exports. At the same time, the strong appreciation of the dollar makes U.S. agricultural exports less competitive in international markets. Because of the overall decline in global agricultural imports neither the United States nor foreign exporters benefit from the changes in trade flows.

Table 8. Exporters in Other Countries of the World Increase Market Share

Commodity	Country/region	High dollar scenario					
		Exports			Imports		
		2010	2015	2017	2010	2015	2017
		Percent change of exports and imports from reference case					
Rice	World	2.6	-2.3	-4.6	2.6	-2.3	-4.6
	World less U.S.	3.2	-1.4	-3.7	2.6	-2.3	-4.7
Wheat	World	0.7	-2.4	-2.2	0.7	-2.4	-2.2
	World less U.S.	1.8	-1.9	-1.6	0.8	-2.4	-2.3
Corn	World	0.0	-6.6	-7.4	0.0	-6.6	-7.4
	World less U.S.	1.3	1.6	2.1	0.0	-6.6	-7.5
Soybeans	World	-0.2	-2.1	-2.0	-0.2	-2.1	-2.0
	World less U.S.	0.6	-0.9	-0.8	-0.2	-2.1	-2.0
Beef and veal	World	-1.1	-7.1	-6.0	-1.1	-7.1	-6.0
	World less U.S.	-1.1	-7.5	-6.1	-1.4	-8.7	-6.8
Pork	World	-0.9	-20.6	-22.6	-0.9	-20.6	-22.6
	World less U.S.	6.0	-1.1	1.8	-1.2	-23.1	-25.3
Poultry	World	-0.6	-11.4	-11.2	-0.6	-11.4	-11.2
	World less U.S.	2.5	5.2	7.4	-0.6	-11.4	-11.2

Source: PEATSim results.

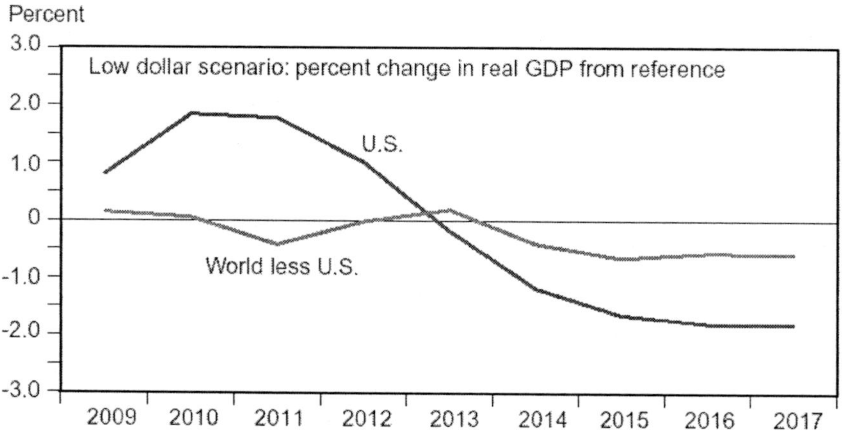

Source: Oxford Economics, December 2008.

Figure 9. U.S. economy slows more than economies of other countries

Low Dollar Scenario: U.S. Agriculture Would Benefit

Turning to the low dollar scenario, the United States' recovery starts out stronger than in the reference case for the first few years of analysis. U.S. real GDP in 2011 is about 2.5 percent higher due to a relatively weaker dollar, resulting in an improved trade balance. U.S. GDP stays above the reference level from 2009-12. However, by 2013 U.S. GDP falls below the reference level and continues to weaken relative to the reference case until the end of the time path, as the U.S. dollar steadily depreciates and consumer savings and investment slows relative to the reference case (figure 9).

Meanwhile, the GDP of other economies around the world tracks relatively closely to the time path for GDP in the reference scenario, fluctuating around the reference scenario by less than half a percent until 2014. By 2015, however, foreign economic growth stabilizes slightly below the reference level. The results by country are mixed. In 2011, in Brazil and Argentina, GDP is 4 and 5 percent lower respectively, while Korea's GDP is almost 5 percent higher than the reference case. While most countries and regions exhibit higher GDP by the end of the scenario, Canada (-5 percent), Mexico (-3 percent), Brazil (-7 percent), Argentina (-13 percent), and even China (-1 percent) and India (-2 percent) experience declines in GDP relative to the reference-level GDP.

In the low dollar scenario, the depreciation of the U.S. dollar leads to higher world agricultural commodity prices (real terms), but as we have seen, the impact on domestic producer prices by country/region is mixed. In some countries, the decrease in demand—due to declines in income—reinforces the effects of cheaper imports on domestic prices leading to a decline in demand for domestic production and a reduction in producer prices below their reference case levels. In other countries, the effects of cheaper imports on domestic prices are offset by increases in demand due to higher incomes (GDP), so producer prices increase.

In the low dollar scenario, exports of other economies outside the United States start out higher for wheat, corn, and beef and veal, as global trade increases due to decline in world prices (table 9). At the end of the time period, in 2017, however, agricultural exports from other economies around the world fall below the reference scenario for all commodities except beef (where there is not much change), as lower economic growth weakens demand.

For the United States, agricultural exports of most products in 2010 are higher compared with the reference case, and remain so through the end of the time path. Even for those commodities where other countries' exports increase against the reference case, their share of world agricultural exports decline. This trend continues over the entire scenario's time period and reflects the increased competitiveness of U.S. agricultural products in world markets from the depreciation of the dollar.

On the import side, foreign (world less United States) agricultural imports of food and feed crops generally trend above the reference level through 2013 (table 10). As the GDP of other economies around the world starts to fall below reference levels, imports of most food and feed crops weaken and fall below levels in the reference scenario by 2015. This decline coincides with lower incomes, weakening demand, and reductions in domestic meat production due to higher levels of relatively cheaper meat imports from the United States. For these other economies, imports of poultry and pork rise from the start and remain substantially above reference levels throughout the projection period. Beef and veal imports rise through 2015, but then fall below the reference level by the end of the projection period in 2017, due primarily to the decline in global GDP.

Table 9. U.S. Exports Benefit from Low Value of Dollar

Commodity	Country/region	Low dollar scenario		
		2010	2015	2017
		Percent change of importsfrom reference case		
Rice	U.S.	0.7	6.6	6.6
	World less U.S.	-1.0	-0.5	-1.7
	World	-0.8	0.3	-0.8
Wheat	U.S.	0.4	1.1	1.1
	World less U.S.	0.8	-1.5	-1.7
	World	0.7	-1.0	-1.2
Corn	U.S.	0.9	0.4	1.4
	World less U.S.	0.2	-0.7	-2.3
	World	0.7	0.0	0.0
Soybeans	U.S.	1.1	13.0	17.6
	World less U.S.	-0.4	-3.7	-4.9
	World	0.0	-0.7	-1.1
Beef and veal	U.S.	0.3	4.1	4.9
	World less U.S.	1.2	1.3	0.1
	World	1.1	1.7	0.7

Source: PEATSim results.

Again, effects for individual countries are mixed. Initially, most countries' imports of grain increase above the reference scenario. Countries with crop imports below their reference scenario level in 2010 include Brazil for wheat and the EU and China for soybeans. At the end of the time path, however, these countries exhibit crop imports below their reference levels.

Table10. Import Growth Slows by 2017

Commodity	Country/region	Low dollar scenario		
		2010	2015	2017
		Percent change of imports from reference case		
Rice	World	-0.8	0.3	-0.8
	World less U.S.	-0.9	0.3	-0.8
Wheat	World	0.7	-1.0	-1.2
	World less U.S.	0.7	-1.0	-1.2
Corn	World	0.7	0.0	0.0
	World less U.S.	0.7	0.0	0.0
Soybeans	World	0.0	-0.7	-1.1
	World less U.S.	0.0	-0.7	-1.1
Beef and veal	World	1.1	1.7	0.7
	World less U.S.	1.4	1.3	-1.1
Pork	World	1.5	6.0	5.3
	World less U.S.	1.7	7.1	6.3
Poultry	World	1.0	5.3	3.2
	World less U.S.	1.0	5.3	3.2

Source: PEATSim results.

THE EFFECTS OF THE GLOBAL ECONOMIC CRISIS ON THE VULNERABLE

The economic crisis and resulting slowdown in global economic growth will have its greatest impacts on international agricultural markets and trade patterns in 2009. The economies of the United States and many industrialized/developed countries are projected to contract sharply. Countries such as China and India, which have experienced high growth rates in the past decade, are likely to continue to have positive income growth but still will experience a substantial slowing of their economies. As a result, the reference level for global GDP in 2009 is expected to decline by 2.0 percent from 2008. Declining global income slows demand which puts downward pressure on agricultural prices, and these lower prices will reduce incentives to production. With declining global income, global consumption growth will slow to less than 0.5 percent for most crops in 2009. The slowing of economic growth and food consumption in lower income countries will likely translate into increases in projected levels of poverty and food insecurity around the world (box 4) as the burgeoning populations of these countries face reduced access to food. Consequently, many of these low-income countries may face financial constraints as they try to meet the food needs of their population in the midst of the economic crisis.

Worldwide Food Insecurity Will Worsen as Global Economic Crisis Deepens

The global economic crisis will likely compound food insecurity in low-income countries and poor households worldwide. The impact of the ongoing economic crisis on food security may not seem disastrous when examining the consequences on a global or national perspective. But indicators of well-being and food security examined at more disaggregated levels strongly suggest that large segments of the population in low-income countries will become more vulnerable.

The slowing of economic growth tends to have a greater impact on food security in poorer countries because of their low per capita incomes and relatively high income inequality (see table below). The inequality in income distribution means that the effect of an economic slowdown will not be felt equally by all. Those in the lowest quintile of the income distribution will be affected the most, and the most negatively. Since the poor in these countries generally spend a much higher share of their income on food than their middle-income and high-income countrymen do, a slowing of economic growth will have a greater impact on the food intake of the poor.

In addition, the growing dependence of low-income countries on food imports will accentuate the impact of the economic crisis on food security. Historical data indicate that developing economies have become increasingly dependent on food imports, including grains, a main staple in their national diets. Their increased reliance on food imports is largely driven by one or a combination of factors: economic growth, trade liberalization, improved transportation systems, slow domestic production growth, and relatively high population growth. Their growing dependency on grain imports renders these low-income countries at greater risk of food insecurity during tough times. In recent years, mounting balance-of-payment deficits, falling revenues from exports, and higher inflation have contributed to a weakening of food-importing countries' capacity to continue importing food at a rate high enough to feed the poor and the very poor in their countries.

The latest long-term food security outlook analysis conducted by the Economic Research Service shows that the developing countries that will be hardest hit by the global economic crisis are those with high levels of balance of payments deficits and high food import dependency. ERS estimates that there will be a 2-percent increase in the number of food-insecure people in 2009. To evaluate the impact of the global economic downturn, the report examines a scenario of reduced capital inflows and export earnings growth in 70 lower income countries. Results indicate the number of food-insecure people would rise by 12 percent from the baseline in 2009.

The report suggests that since most of these poor countries do not have the resources to assist the vulnerable segments of their populations, there will be continued need for food assistance from the more developed economies.

For more details, see the ERS report, Food Security Assessment, 2008-09, available at: www.ers.usda.gov/publications/gfa20/.

Commercial grain imports are growing in 70 developing countries

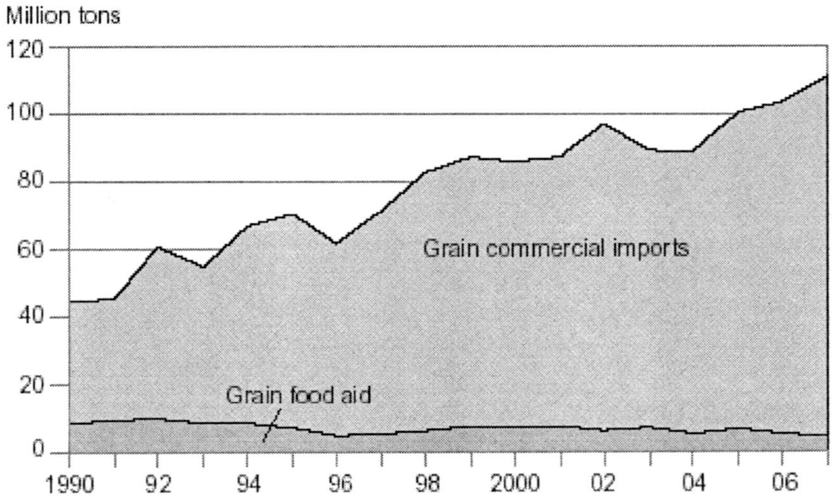

Source: United Nations, FAOSTAT. For list of 70 countries, please see: www.ers.usda.gov/publications/GFA20/

Global economic crisis compounds food insecurity in developing countries

Country/ region	2008 GDP per capita per year	2008 GDP per capita per day	Gini coeff.[1] measure of income inequality	Share of food to total consumer spending on goods and services	Average daily caloric intake 2003-05	Undernourished population 2003-05	Daily deficit of undernourished population 2003-05
	2000 US$			*Percent*	*Kilocalories per person*	*Percent*	*Kilocalories per person*
United States	38,952	107	0.41	13.7	3,770	< 1	100
Japan	20,112	55	0.25	19.8	2,770	< 1	140
Canada	26,370	72	0.32	18.0	3,590	< 1	110
South Korea	15,038	41	0.35	23.1	3,030	< 1	130
China	1,922	5.3	0.47	39.8	2,990	9	240
India	707	1.9	0.37	49.5	2,360	21	260
Mexico	6,482	18	0.51	34.0	3,270	5	190
Argen-tina	9,459	26	0.49	33.4	3,000	< 1	130
Brazil	4,315	12	0.57	20.8	3,090	12	220
Madagas car	260	0.7	0.48	71.8	2,010	37	290
Zambia	413	1.1	0.51	64.0	1,890	45	330
Bangla-desh	458	1.3	0.33	53.8	2,230	27	290

[1]The Gini coefficient measures the inequality of income distribution within a country.

Source: United Nations Food and Agriculture Organization (FAO) statistical yearbook; FAO, *The State of Food Insecurity in the World* (SOFI) reports; USDA, ERS International Macro Data Set.

CONCLUSION

The world financial (economic) crisis of 2008-09 is the most serious world recession since the 1930s. While the impact on the United States is not as serious as in the Great Depression, the extent of the global recession and the number of countries involved is unique. This crisis, like all major economic events, will have profound impacts on the economies around the world. The short-term impact (caused by reduced demand) is a major decline in the value of both merchandise and agricultural commodity trade. Much of the decline in the value of trade has come from declining prices, but there are also declines in the volume of trade. The longer term impacts of the crisis will depend on the adjustment path to resolve the imbalances that have emerged in global trade and savings.

Substantial imbalances that led to the crisis have emerged between trade-surplus countries such as China and trade-deficit countries such as the United States. If the resolution of the crisis is an exchange-rate realignment which reduces the trade and savings imbalances and leads to a more sustainable world economic growth path, then the longer term outlook for renewed growth and prosperity is quite good. If on the other hand, the realignment in exchange rates leads to continued or widening trade and savings imbalances, the global adjustment is just being put off for another day, and future crises are likely. The realignment that would result in reduced imbalances involves the currencies of trade-surplus countries outside of the United States appreciating in real terms. This implies that the U.S. dollar will depreciate in real terms against both its trading partners and its competitors. A relatively low dollar has always been favorable to U.S. agriculture, providing robust export growth and relatively high agricultural commodity prices. In this sense, there is a confluence of interests between the agricultural sector and the global resolution of the crisis toward a more sustainable world economic growth path.

While the sustainable resolution of the crisis on a macroeconomic level implies reducing global imbalances, that resolution will also imply substantial changes to both the commodity composition of trade and the major markets for U.S. agricultural exports. On the commodity side, it is likely that there will be an acceleration of the movement toward higher value trade, particularly trade in meats and feed grains.

In the short term, the slowing of income growth in developing countries will likely lead to increases in food insecurity and poverty around the world. Income growth, however, is expected to rebound in most countries by the end of 2010 and continue to grow for several years through 2012 before stabilizing around its new longrun trend growth rates. As a result, agricultural imports, after declining in 2009, are likely to continue to grow into the future.

The continued strength of global agricultural imports is primarily a result of the growth of consumption in emerging and developing countries and the increase in meat consumption among those countries' consumers. Even during the initial period of the economic crisis and its recovery, economic growth in those countries remains positive and relatively strong. As a result, their consumption of food is likely to increase and trade in meat and feed grains will likely grow faster than trade in food grains. Over the longer term, the most likely path of recovery for the global economy indicates that the growth in consumption and imports of agricultural products by emerging and developing countries will remain strong.

REFERENCES

Childs, Nathan & James Kiawu. (2009). *Factors Behind the Rise in Global Rice Prices in 2008*, USDA, Economic Research Service, Outlook Report No. RCS-09D-01.. Available at: *www.ers.usda.gov/Publications/* RCS/May09/RCS09D01/.

Dirkse, Steve & M.C. Ferris. (1995). "The Path Solver: A Non-monotone Stabilization Scheme for Mixed Complementarity Problems," *Optimization Methods and Software*, pp. 123-156.

IHS Global Insight. Interim forecast spreadsheet. Cambridge. MA. 2009.

Langley, Suchada, report coordinator. *International Financial Crises and Agriculture*. USDA, Economic Research Service, Outlook Report No. WRS-99-3. 2000. Available at: http://usda.mannlib.cornell.edu/usda/ers/WRS//2000s/2000/WRS-03-07-2000_International_Financial_Crisis.pdf.

Oxford Economics. (2008). *Oxford Macroeconomic Forecasting Model*. December 18, release.

Peters, May, Agapi Somwaru, James Hansen, Ralph Seeley, and Steve Dirkse. *Modeling Biofuels Expansion in a Changing Global Environment.* Research paper presented at the International Association of Agricultural Economics Triennial Conference. Beijing, China. August 16-22, 2009. Available at: http://ageconsearch.umn.edu/handle/51732/.

Shane, Mathew, Terry Roe, and Agapi Somwaru. "Exchange Rates, Foreign Income, and U.S. Agricultural Exports," *Agricultural and Resource Economics Review*, 37/2, pp. 160-175. October 2008.

Shane, Mathew & David Stallings. (1987). *The World Debt Crisis and Its Resolution*, USDA, Economic Research Service, Foreign Agricultural Economic Report No. 231.

Shane, Mathew, William Liefert, Mitch Morehart, May Peters, John Dillard, David Torgerson, and Bill Edmondson. *The 2008/2009 World Economic Crisis: What It Means for U.S. Agriculture*. USDA, Economic Research Service, Outlook Report No. WRS-09-02, March 2009. Available at:

www. ers.usda.gov/Publications/WRS0902/.

Shapouri, Shahla, Stacey Rosen, Birgit Meade & Fred Gale. (2009) *Food Security Assessment, 2008-09*. USDA, Economic Research Service, Outlook Report No. GFA-20, June. Available at: *www.ers.usda.gov/* Publications/gfa20/.

United Nations Food and Agriculture Organization. (2008). *The State of Food Insecurity in the World* (SOFI). Available at: http://www.fao.org/ docrep/011/i0291e/i0291e00.htm/.

United Nations Food and Agriculture Organization. FAOSTAT database. 2009. Available at: http://faostat.fao.org/.

U.S. Department of Agriculture, Economic Research Service, Agricultural Exchange Rate Data Set. (2009). Available at: www.ers.usda.gov/ Data/ ExchangeRates/.

U.S. Department of Agriculture, Economic Research Service, International Macroeconomic Data Set. (2009). Available at: www.ers.usda.gov/Data/ Macroeconomics/.

U.S. Department of Agriculture, Foreign Agricultural Trade of the United States (FATUS) data set. (2009). Available at: *www.ers.usda.* gov/Data/FATUS/.

U.S. Department of Agriculture, Office of the Chief Economist. *USDA Agricultural Projections to 2017*, Report No. OCE-2008-1. 2008. Available at: www.ers.usda.gov/Publications/OCE081/.

U.S. Department of Commerce, U.S. Census Bureau, *Current Population Survey*. (2008). Available at: http://www.census.gov/cps/.

World Atlas. (2009). *World Trade Atlas, International Division*. Global Trade Information Services, Inc. Database accessed April. Available at: http://www. gtis.com/.

End Notes

[1] Most economists agree that negative gross domestic product (GDP) growth over more than two quarters qualifies as a recession.

[2] Many forecasts continue to indicate that economic recovery is likely to occur toward the last quarter of 2009 or first quarter of 2010.

[3] The European Union is comprised of 27 member countries: Austria, Belgium, Bulgaria, Cyprus, the Czech Republic, Denmark, Estonia, Finland, France, Germany, Greece, Hungary, Ireland, Italy, Latvia, Lithuania, Luxembourg, Malta, Netherlands, Poland, Portugal, Romania, Slovakia, Slovenia, Spain, Sweden, and the United Kingdom. The PEATSim model covers all EU-27 member countries except Bulgaria and Romania.

In: Impact of Global Economic Crisis ... ISBN: 978-1-61761-180-3
Editor: Austen W. Young

Chapter 2

THE 2008/2009 WORLD ECONOMIC CRISIS: WHAT IT MEANS FOR U.S. AGRICULTURE

Mathew Shane, William Liefert, Mitch Morehart, May Peters, John Dillard, David Torgerson and William Edmondson

ABSTRACT

The world economic crisis that began in 2008 has major consequences for U.S. agriculture. The weakening of global demand because of emerging recessions and declining economic growth result in reduced export demand and lower agricultural commodity prices, compared with those in 2008. These, in turn, reduce U.S. farm income and place downward pressure on farm real estate values. So far, the overall impact on U.S. agriculture is not as severe as on the broader U.S. economy because the record-high agricultural exports, prices, and farm income in 2007 and 2008 put U.S. farmers on solid financial ground. Moreover, the debt equity ratios in agriculture tend to be more conservative than those in most other sectors of the economy. There is much uncertainty concerning the depth and extent of the crisis. The outcomes for U.S. agriculture depend on whether or not there is a global realignment of exchange rates to correct current macroeconomic imbalances.

Keywords: world economic crisis, U.S. agriculture, U.S. agricultural exports, agricultural commodity prices, U.S. trade-weighted exchange rate, U.S. farm income

ACKNOWLEDGMENTS

The authors would like to acknowledge the support and assistance of Janet Perry of USDA's Economic Research Service (ERS), who helped coordinate the production of the report. We appreciate the contributions of Ed Young and Mary Ahearn, ERS, to the sections on farm programs and farm household income. We would like to thank all of the reviewers for their helpful comments and suggestions, including Terry Roe, University of Minnesota; David Orden, International Food Policy Research Institute; Jason Henderson, Federal Reserve Bank of Kansas City; Josef Schmidhuber, Global Perspective Studies Unit of the Food and Agriculture Organization of the United Nations; Daniel Whitley, USDA's Foreign Agricultural Service; and Cheryl Christensen, Barry Krissoff, Suchada Langley, and Sally Thompson, ERS. We also appreciate and acknowledge the editorial and design assistance of John Weber and Cynthia Ray.

SUMMARY

The 2008-09 world economic crisis has major impacts on U.S. agriculture. Declining incomes around the world as a result of the evolving worldwide recession combined with the short-term appreciation of the dollar result in significant declines in U.S. agricultural exports and sharply lower agricultural prices, farm income, and employment, compared with those in 2007-08. Agricultural households also suffer from declining income from off-farm jobs, as the economic recession in the United States ripples through to rural- based businesses and loss of tax revenue puts pressure on rural government employment and social services. Because the U.S. farm sector went into the crisis with record-high exports, prices, and farm income, the declines, although substantial, will bring agriculture back to trend outcomes. While there is a great deal of uncertainty concerning the full magnitude of the U.S. and global recession, the effects of the crisis are expected to be less severe for U.S. agriculture than for many other sectors of the U.S. economy.

In 2007 and 2008, U.S. net farm income equaled $87 billion and $89 billion, respectively, with each year establishing a new nominal record. Even when adjusted for inflation, these amounts reflect the highest net farm incomes since the early 1970s. Depending on assumptions about the extent of the economic downturn, this analysis projects that U.S. net farm income in 2009 could fall by 26 percent to $66 billion—a level similar to the average of $65 billion earned in the previous 10 years—and in the worst case scenario to $60 billion (a drop of 33 percent).

The projected decline in farm income in 2009 is not expected to have much effect on national agricultural land values. Land value trends that emerged in 2008 could continue in States that showed the largest declines in rural housing values and abate in States that enjoyed double-digit increases in land values due to strong crop receipts.[1] The economic crisis could also reduce U.S. agricultural export-related employment in the short run, as projected 2009 employment falls by 13 percent (a loss of 45,000 jobs).

The crisis will impact U.S. agriculture mostly through indirect international effects rather than through changes in the U.S. economy. The slowdown of growth in foreign economies will reduce import demand for agricultural commodities, resulting in lower U.S. agricultural exports and prices for agricultural commodities. Although the crisis originated in the United States, it has spread to the rest of the world and, especially, to large emerging markets, such as China, South Korea, and Mexico. The crisis is also strengthening the dollar against most other foreign currencies, as money throughout the world flows into the United States as a safe haven. In 2008, the net inflow of capital to the United States totaled about $650 billion. The stronger dollar reduces U.S. agricultural exports by making them more expensive in foreign markets than output by competitors. This analysis suggests that as a consequence of the slowing global economy and the appreciation of the dollar, U.S. agricultural exports could fall from $117 billion in 2008 to $96 billion in 2009.

Another feature of the crisis is that declining world economic activity has caused world energy prices to decline precipitously. This will not affect U.S. agricultural producers uniformly. The fall in energy prices has reduced the price and profitability of biofuels, and thereby lowered prices for feedstock crops, especially corn. On the other hand, all producers will benefit from lower input costs implied by reduced energy and fuel prices. This report projects that in 2009, the fuel and energy-related input costs faced by U.S. farmers could decline by 30 percent, returning costs to the levels of 2006. Livestock producers will be net beneficiaries of the energy price drop, as the decrease in crop prices will lower their feed costs.

Macroeconomic forecasters, such as Global Insight and EIU, predict that the U.S. and world economies should stabilize in 2010 and then resume growth in 2011 near the relatively high rates of the early 2000s.[2] The return to a growing world gross domestic product and consumer income, especially in emerging markets, will lead to a recovery in U.S. agricultural exports. Thus, this report's reference analysis[3] projects that by 2013, U.S. net farm income could rise to $83 billion, though agricultural exports are projected to be only $93 billion, largely unchanged from the projected 2009 value of $96 billion because of the higher value of the dollar. The return to growth will also expand demand for energy. This shift suggests that world energy and fuel prices could again increase. Economic growth would partially reverse the effects of the crisis and thereby help producers of corn and other biofuel feedstock crops. Effects on the livestock sector will be positive because of the economic growth but negative because of rising costs for feed and energy.

The main uncertainty for the long run concerns the value of the U.S. dollar compared with currencies of other major trading countries. One possibility is that the dollar will continue to strengthen substantially, especially against the Chinese yuan and currencies of other major emerging markets. Another is that the dollar will weaken, as it did doing during most of the 2000s before the 2008 crisis. In the first scenario, U.S. farmers will face a stronger dollar, which will reduce the price competitiveness of U.S. agricultural exports. In the appreciating dollar scenario, U.S. net farm income will decline by almost 7 percent to $83 billion and agricultural exports will drop by 27 percent to $85 billion by 2013. In the second scenario, the weaker dollar relative to the reference case will strengthen U.S. farmers' competitiveness on world markets. With a weaker dollar, projected net farm income will increase by 19 percent to $106 billion in 2013 and to $118 billion in 2017, while agricultural exports will rise to $120 billion in 2013 and $134 billion in 2017. The weaker dollar, combined with the return to world growth, will create strong foreign demand for U.S. agricultural goods, which will help keep farm income high.

INTRODUCTION

In the years leading up to the economic crisis that began in 2008, the global economy showed strong growth. Over 2001-07, real world gross domestic product (GDP) grew by more than 3 percent a year, exceeding annual growth of 2.7 percent during the 1990s (figure 1). Emerging market economies, including China, India, and Russia, expanded at an especially high 6 percent a year, in part because of economic reforms enacted over the past two decades. U.S. agriculture benefited from rising world prosperity, which resulted in growth in U.S. agricultural exports to record-high levels and historically high agricultural commodity prices. Combined, these factors contributed to growth of 43 percent in real (inflation-adjusted) farm income over 2000-07 (ERS, 2009b).[4]

Agriculture has always been a heavily trade-dependent sector. In 2007, the farm share of U.S. economic activity generated by agricultural exports was 27 percent, or nearly $57 billion. In the same period, bulk commodities accounted for 40 percent of U.S. agricultural exports, and high-value products accounted for 60 percent.[5] Almost 20 percent of the economic activity generated by high-value exports was attributed to processes done on farms (Edmondson, 2008b).[6]

The financial crisis began in the United States in mid-2007 with increasing interest rate spreads and declining house prices, and in September 2007, the injection of liquidity into financial markets by the Federal Reserve, Bank of England, and the European Central Bank. The financial crisis quickly spread throughout the U.S. economy and the rest of the world and by the second half of 2008 resulted in recessions in numerous countries. How might the financial crisis and ensuing economic recession (hereinafter, the economic crisis) affect U.S. agriculture, especially given that agricultural exports account for around 20 percent of the value of U.S. agricultural production?[7] To address the question, this analysis uses models to project U.S. agricultural exports, prices, farm income, agricultural employment, and farm real estate values out to 2017. Projections are based on two alternative scenarios that reflect different assumptions about the depth of the recession and alternative outcomes for the value of the dollar compared with the currencies of U.S. major agricultural trading partners.

Causes of the Economic Crisis

The 2008/2009 world economic crisis was caused mainly by a combination of world macroeconomic imbalances and severe weaknesses in the U.S. and Western financial system.[8] Since the mid-1990s, world economic growth has involved major macroeconomic imbalances between two different groups of countries, mainly the United States and Great Britain on one hand and various Asian countries, such as China, South Korea, and Taiwan, referred to as "trade surplus" countries, on the other (see Wolf, 2008; Council of Economic Advisors, 2009). The United States saved less as a share of its GDP and consumed more, compared with the trade surplus countries. At the expense of domestic consumption, the trade surplus countries expanded production and exports and, in the process, accumulated huge holdings of foreign exchange denominated in currencies of their major export markets (especially the United States).

The imbalances became self-sustaining. The United States ran large negative trade balances, and the surplus countries large positive balances (Federal Reserve Board, 2009). The surplus countries, in turn, lent the United States a large share of their accumulated foreign exchange reserves (mostly by buying U.S. Treasury bills). These reverse capital flows helped finance U.S. trade deficits, while at the same time kept the currencies of the trade surplus countries from rising in value (appreciating) against the dollar (Wolf, 2008). The capital inflows lowered U.S. interest rates and increased business investment, boosting GDP, consumption, and imports. The capital inflows also expanded investment in equities and property, which contributed to an asset price boom. The rise in asset prices increased consumer wealth, which further stimulated U.S. consumption spending and imports, and thereby helped sustain the trade deficit.

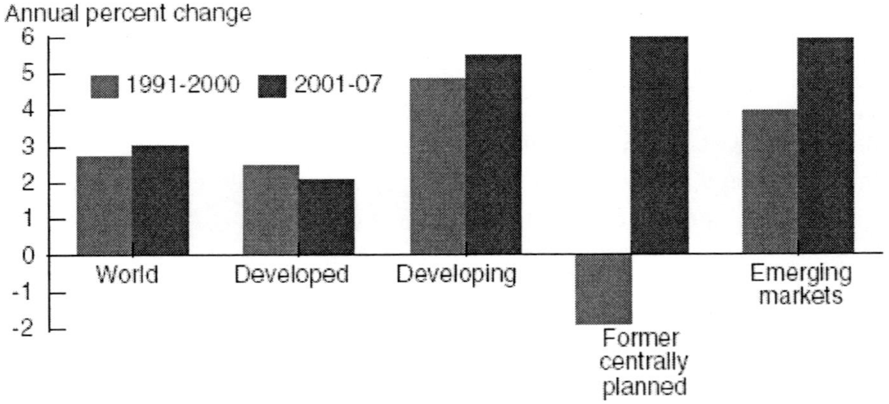

Source: USDA, Economic Research Service, International Macroeconomic Data Set.

Figure 1. Real GDP growth rates *Growth imbalance put pressure on resource supplies*

The large influx of money into the Western financial system enlarged the supply of funds available for loans and investment relative to the profitable opportunities available. This consequence, combined with insufficient government financial regulation and supervision, resulted in investors and banks making riskier loans, such as for subprime home mortgages and mortgage refinancing in the Unites States. The increase in delinquent loans for U.S. home mortgages in 2007-08 precipitated the U.S. financial crisis, as financial institutions' liability to asset ratios began to deteriorate.

Another cause of the economic crisis was innovative practices used in the financial markets during the 1990s and 2000s, which had the effect of reducing transparency and increasing risk (Lewis, 2008; Council of Economic Advisors, 2009). The securitization (bundling) of different types of loans and development of other new financial products (such as mortgage- backed securities, loan default swaps, and collateralized debt obligations) lowered transparency. To maximize shortrun gains, financial firms became highly leveraged by keeping their reserves low relative to the magnitude of funds lent or invested.

As the home mortgage delinquency rate increased, securitization and other derivative products made it difficult for lenders to assess their own exposure and that of potential borrowers to bad debt. After the collapse of the global financial services firm Lehman Brothers in September 2008, lending among banks and other financial firms was sharply curtailed and interest rate risk premiums rose rapidly. Because financial institutions could not borrow easily from secondary financial markets to raise funds, they had to sell assets. This led to substantial discounting of bonds and rapid price declines in equity markets. All these problems were compounded by financial firms' earlier extreme leveraging of funds. Given the openness of U.S. financial markets and the heavy participation of foreign banks and financial firms in those markets, the U.S. financial crisis quickly spread throughout the world (Krugman, 2008).

As their liability to asset holding deteriorated further, financial institutions became more conservative in their lending practices. This disruption to lending began hurting business investment, the housing market, consumer durable spending (such as for automobiles and appliances), and employment. The drop in asset values (equities, property) throughout the world has sharply reduced consumer wealth, also causing consumer spending to fall. The declines in investment and consumption are driving the current world economic downturn.

Direct Effects of the Economic Crisis on U.S. Agriculture

The economic crisis will have direct and indirect effects on U.S. agriculture. The direct effects will come from changes within the U.S. economy. The indirect effects will stem from the impacts of the crisis on foreign income, trade, and world energy prices.

The direct effect of the crisis on U.S. agriculture is expected to be modest. On the demand side, the crisis is likely to lower U.S. GDP (Global Insight (2009) projects a decline of 2.7 percent in 2009), and thereby consumer spending on food. This demand effect, though, will probably be small. Most U.S. consumers have a sufficiently high standard of living that demand for food is not very sensitive to changes in income.[9] Consumers are less likely to eat out at restaurants, and an increasing share may choose to shop for food at warehouse outlets. Total consumer expenditures on food (including food away from home) will fall, but the amount of food actually consumed will not. This will likely result in a changing composition of demand for agricultural commodities and products and, thereby, a fall in some agricultural prices. For example, demand may shift from more expensive beef and fish to less expensive meats, such as poultry. Consumers may also reduce purchases of "organic" foods in favor of more "industrial" foods.

On the supply side, the disruption of overall U.S. financial markets could inhibit lending to farmers and agribusinesses. Agribusinesses heavily dependent on credit could be constrained, which, in turn, could lower demand for agricultural inputs. In recent years, farm borrowing has increased from large regional banks, some of which have moved toward riskier lending behavior (FDIC, 2008). Yet, most rural banks that lend to farmers are not closely tied to the financial world that created, and is now suffering from, the financial crisis. Agricultural borrowers and lenders tend to have secure long-term relationships, which should mitigate the crisis's effect on the flow of loans to farmers.

Indirect Effects of the Economic Crisis on U.S. Agriculture

The main indirect effects of the crisis will come from its impacts on GDP and income in overseas markets, especially in countries that are large importers of U.S. agricultural goods; on energy prices (which are falling because of the decline in world economic activity); and on the exchange rate of the U.S. dollar against foreign currencies. While it has been shown that foreign income and exchange rates are major determinants of levels of U.S. agricultural exports, their impacts on high-value products differ significantly from those on bulk commodities (Shane et al., 2008). U.S. agricultural exports of high-value agricultural products tend to be more sensitive to changes in foreign income growth and less sensitive to exchange rate changes than those of bulk commodity exports.

GDP

The spread of the economic crisis beyond the United States will hurt economic growth throughout the world. Oxford Economic Forecasting (2009) projects that world GDP in 2009 will fall by more than 2 percent. The last time world growth was negative was 1982. Negative world growth in 2009 will be down from a rate of about 2.5 percent in 2008 and the 3-percent yearly average since 1970. Like the United States, many countries are projected to have recessions with declines in GDP. Although demand for food in the United States and other wealthier developed countries is highly unresponsive to changes in consumer income, this is not the case for developing countries. A major contraction in these countries' GDP could cut spending on food and industrial demand for agricultural products substantially. Countries that are large markets for U.S. agriculture could reduce their imports. By the end of 2008, there was evidence that this was already happening in China, Taiwan, Mexico, Egypt, and Russia (FATUS, March 2009).

Just as high world economic growth during the 2000s contributed to the spike in world energy prices in 2007-08, the economic crisis's negative effect on growth is contributing to the drop in demand and prices for energy. After peaking at $147 a barrel in July 2008, the price of oil plunged to $32 a barrel at the beginning of 2009 (EIA, 2008; 2009).

The fall in energy prices will have a negative demand-side effect and positive supply-side effect on farmers. The negative effect is that prices for biofuels, and thereby for biofuel feedstocks, will drop, which will impact producers of bulk crops (especially corn in the United States). For example, from July 2008 to January 2009, the price of ethanol decreased from $2.90 a gallon to $1.61 (ERS, 2009a), and the price of corn correspondingly dropped from a peak of over $7 in summer 2008 to less than $4 in January 2009. A positive effect for agriculture is that prices are also likely to decline for energy- based agricultural inputs, such as gasoline, diesel, and electricity. Decreasing natural gas prices are also likely to put downward pressure on fertilizer prices. For U.S. bulk crop producers, energy-based inputs can account for half to two-thirds of operating costs, and one-sixth to one-third of total costs (ERS, 2009b).

The drop in energy prices will not affect all U.S. agricultural producers uniformly. All farmers will benefit from the price decrease for energy-based inputs. Yet, crop producers who sell biofuel feedstock will see their output prices fall and will probably be net losers (just as they were net gainers from the surge in energy prices over 2007-08). On the other hand, producers of meat and other livestock products will especially benefit, as prices will decrease not only for their energy-based inputs but also for their animal feed.

Exchange Rate of the Dollar

Another major indirect effect of the world economic crisis on U.S. agriculture will be the degree to which the value of the dollar reacts against the currencies of developing countries that are large importers of U.S. agricultural goods. Predicting this effect is challenging.

As discussed earlier, one of the main causes of the economic crisis was the macroeconomic imbalances that accompanied world growth, in particular that the United States saved too little and consumed too much, compared with the trade surplus countries of Asia. These imbalances could be corrected by a realignment of exchange rates involving an appreciation of the surplus countries' currencies against the dollar. This would raise the prices of their exports in the United States and lower the prices of U.S. exports in their countries. U.S. imports and consumption would fall and exports to trade surplus countries rise, while trade surplus country exports would drop and their imports and consumption rise. The U.S. trade deficit would shrink. In the early and mid-2000s, exchange rates in fact moved in this direction. For example, between 2005 and 2008, the dollar depreciated against the Chinese yuan by 18 percent in real terms (after correcting for infl ation) (figure 2); between 2001 and 2007, it depreciated against the South Korean won by 40 percent (real terms); and between 2002 and 2008, the dollar fell in real terms against all foreign currencies by 17 percent.[10]

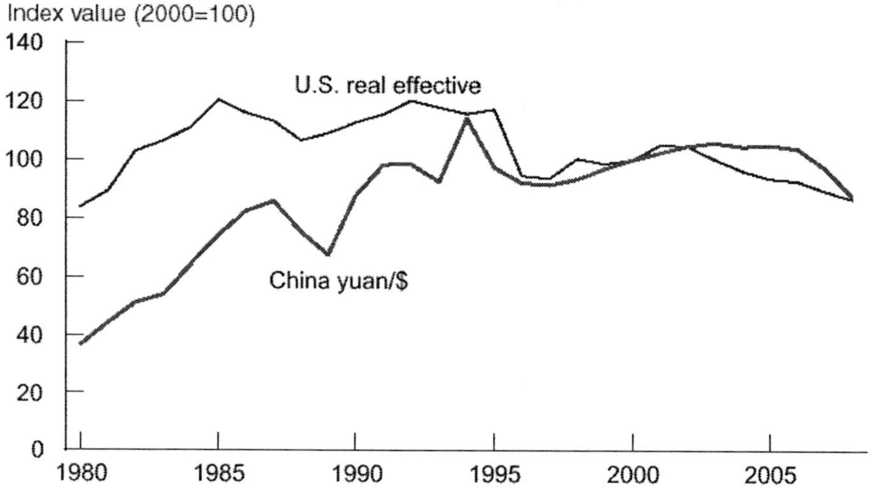

Note: Indexes are calculated based on foreign currency per U.S. dollar.
Source: USDA, Economic Research Service, International Macroeconomic Data Set.

Figure 2. China's and U.S. real exchange rate *China's real exchange rate has appreciated since 2005*

Yet, the crisis's shortrun effect on the dollar has been to appreciate it rather than depreciate it against the Chinese yuan and most other currencies. Although the crisis originated in the United States, financial investment here (whether in U.S. government securities or bank financial instruments) is considered less risky than in most other countries, so money throughout the world is seeking a safe haven from uncertain conditions around the world. From July to December 2008, the dollar appreciated overall in real terms by 17 percent (ERS, 2009d), and ERS projects that in 2009, the dollar will increase in real terms by a further 5 percent.

The inflow of funds to the United States has the benefit of helping the U.S. government finance the policies needed to stimulate the economy, to the advantage of the entire world. On the other hand, the dollar appreciation is delaying the correction of the world macroeconomic imbalances that helped spawn the economic crisis. The dollar is appreciating against the currencies of most other countries, developed as well as developing. This means the appreciation is making U.S. agricultural exports less price competitive than output produced not only by importing countries but also by exporting competitors, such as Canada, Australia, and Brazil.

If the United States has a comparative advantage in the structure of its capital markets, then a relatively weak global economy in the intermediate term is likely to result in continued capital inflows and appreciation of the dollar. This would suggest a greater need to balance the fiscal budget in the long term so that foreign savings go into private capital markets. These developments eventually would lead to lower interest rates, higher investment, and incentives for foreign savings to go to other world markets.

This study investigates two longer term scenarios involving the dollar's exchange rate. The first is that the dollar continues to appreciate against the currencies of other countries with which the United States has large trade deficits. Trade surplus countries continue to invest the dollars they earn from their U.S. positive trade balance back into the United States. By keeping the dollar strong, this behavior would prevent market forces from eliminating the U.S. trade deficit through dollar depreciation. In this scenario, the world could rebound from the economic crisis, with the U.S financial system strengthened, though with the same general patterns of growth and trade as before. U.S. agriculture would benefit from resumed world growth, but without the benefit that could have come from dollar depreciation.

In this dollar appreciation scenario, the macroeconomic imbalances between the United States and the trade surplus countries go uncorrected for the long run as well as for the short run. The scenario carries the risk of an equally or even more serious economic crisis in the future. The crisis could be sparked not by weaknesses within the world financial system but rather by worries about the post-recovery sustainability of the dollar's value, which might trigger large-scale capital flight from the United States. The United States could have an economic crisis similar to that of various emerging market economies during the last 15 years, such as Thailand and Indonesia in the late 1 990s, which could pull down the entire world economy.

The second scenario is that the dollar depreciates against the trade surplus country currencies. Trade surplus countries reduce their investment of excess dollars accumulated from U.S. trade into the United States, which results in a depreciation of the dollar and a declining U.S. trade deficit. The low dollar scenario would result in a significant reduction of global macroeconomic imbalances and could lead to sustainable world economic growth. In this scenario, U.S. agriculture would benefit doubly from renewed world growth and dollar depreciation, both of which would increase foreign demand for U.S. products and also put upward pressure on agricultural commodity prices (see box, " Uncertainty Concerning the Economic Crisis").

Uncertainty Concerning the Economic Crisis

Economists and others continue to be uncertain as to the length and depth of the economic crisis both in the United States and abroad. Forecasts of the crisis's effect on GDP in the United States and other countries are being revised downward on a monthly basis. One reason for the uncertainty is that the forecasts are based on models that assume that markets work well, if not perfectly. Key features of the financial crisis are that information about credit risk is difficult or impossible to obtain, and confidence in U.S. and world financial markets has eroded. Consequently, these markets are working poorly, which hurts all other economic activity.

Another element of uncertainty is the degree to which the decline of confidence in the economy will reduce consumer spending. A "paradox of thrift" could occur whereby the apparently prudent decision of individual households to consume less and save more creates a downward spiral of falling consumer demand, which lowers GDP, employment, and income, which reduces spending. The longrun correction of the world macroeconomic imbalances that helped create the economic crisis requires that consumers in the United States and certain other countries consume less and save more. Yet, too strong an adjustment in that direction in the short run could deepen the economic crisis. This point is also relevant for assessing model-based macro forecasts of the crisis's impact on consumption spending and GDP. Consumers' actual propensities to consume and save could be changing currently from the parameter values measuring these behaviors that are embedded in the models.

Another element of uncertainty is whether the Asian trade surplus countries that (unlike the United States) have had large savings will begin to spend more of their accumulated wealth. If and when this happens, it would have an expansionary effect on production and income growth around the world, to the benefit of U.S. agricultural exports.

Model Projections of the Crisis's Effects on U.S. Agriculture

This ERS analysis uses a number of different modeling frameworks to generate the full set of projections. The Oxford Global Macroeconomic Model is used to produce a consistent set of macroeconomic assumptions for the various scenarios. The ERS PEATSim modeling framework of world agricultural trade incorporates the implications of these assumptions to generate projections for the crisis's effects on U.S. and world agricultural commodity markets: world agricultural prices, production, consumption, and trade (see boxes, "Oxford Global Macroeconomic Model" and "ERS PEATSim Model"). The ERS models for U.S. farm income, agricultural employment, and real estate values then use the PEATSim results to generate projections for those variables.

Model projections are first presented for the crisis's impact on U.S. agricultural exports and world prices, and then on U.S. farm income, agricultural employment, and real estate values. The degree to which the crisis affects U.S. agriculture—farm income, employment, and real estate values—will be driven by the impacts of the crisis on U.S. agricultural exports and the demand for biofuel feedstocks.

OXFORD GLOBAL MACROECONOMIC MODEL

The Oxford Economic Forecasting Global Macroeconomic model is a quarterly dynamic international econometric model. It covers 76 countries, with primary models for 44 countries and secondary models for 32 others. Data are imbedded in the model for a wide variety of macroeconomic variables going back to 1970, and the model generates projections out to 10 years. The model is updated every month, and a new base projection is run. For major countries such as the United States, the underlying database contains about 450 variables. For secondary countries, the variable coverage is smaller. The model is designed to be user friendly.

The Oxford model is used to generate the projected values of countries' GDP, exchange rates, inflation rates (as measured by the consumer price index), GDP defl ator, the world price of oil, and interest rates, which are then entered into USDA's PEATSim model. The various macroeconomic scenarios are produced by changing a key variable, computing a new solution, and comparing the new results with those of the base run (the reference scenario). Charting and tabling tools are available to evaluate the scenarios.

The macroeconomic assumptions used in all three projection scenarios (including the reference scenario) differ from those that underpin the *USDA Agricultural Projections to 2018*, which means that the projections made in this report for U.S. agricultural exports, prices, and other market effects also differ from those in the *USDA Agricultural Projections to 2018*. The macroeconomic assumptions for the USDA baseline were made in October 2008, while the assumptions for this report were made in January 2009, when the empirical evidence indicated that the world economic crisis would be more severe than was thought in mid- autumn 2008.

ERS PEATSIM MODEL

The Partial Equilibrium Agricultural Trade Simulation model, or PEATSim, is a dynamic, partial equilibrium, multicommodity, multiregion global gross trade model of the agriculture sector. It uses supply and demand equations to capture the economic behavior of producers, consumers, and markets in a global framework. It includes variables for production, acreage, yields, consumption, exports, imports, stocks, world prices, and domestic producer prices. Identities such as supply and utilization, consumption, and its components hold for all commodities and regions in the model. The model calibrates each country's agricultural activities to USDA's long-term projections (USDA, 2008). The model balances global supply and demand. Prices are determined at levels that permit global market equilibrium to be achieved.

PEATSim covers 37 agricultural commodities: 12 crops—rice, wheat, corn, other coarse grains, soybeans, sunflowers, rapeseed, peanuts, cotton, other oilseeds, tropical oils, and sugar; 12 oilseed oil and meal products—from soybeans, sunflowerseed, rapeseed, cottonseed, peanuts, and other oilseeds; 4 livestock products—beef and veal, pork, poultry, and raw milk; 6 dairy products—fluid milk, butter, cheese, nonfat dry milk, whole dry milk, and other dairy products; and 3 biofuel commodities and byproducts—ethanol, biodiesel, and dried distillers' grains.

PEATSim includes 13 countries or regions—the United States, the European Union, Canada, Mexico, Japan, South Korea, Australia, New Zealand, China, Brazil, Argentina, India, and the rest of the world (ROW).

PEATSim can model country-specific trade and domestic policies. It is written in GAMS (General Algebraic Modeling System) and uses a Mixed Complementarity Problem (MCP) solver that allows it to handle different production-consumption regimes and functional form discontinuities. The model's innovative and flexible specification enables it to analyze a variety of scenarios. Model solutions provide information on changes in prices, consumption, production, imports, and exports.

Reference projections are made from 2009 to 2017. Both short- and longrun projections are discussed. The short run is defined as the next 1-3 years (2009-11). The crisis's projected effects depend on assumptions made for the future values of key macroeconomic variables, such as countries' GDP, exchange rates, inflation rates, and the world price of oil. Because of the uncertainty concerning the future path of the value of the dollar (appreciation versus depreciation), this analysis makes different assumptions concerning the dollar's future exchange rate (figure 3). These assumptions generate different scenarios for the crisis's effects on U.S. agriculture.

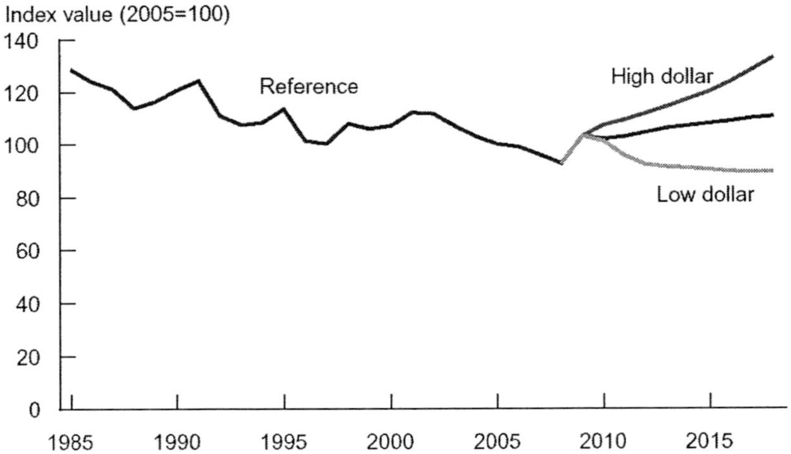

Source: USDA, Economic Research Service (ERS), International Macroeconomic Data Set; ERS projections.

Figure 3. The U.S. trade-weighted exchange rate under alternative scenarios *Exchange rate changes are important for U.S. agriculture*

In the reference scenario, it is assumed here that the dollar appreciates moderately after 2009 in real terms over both the short run and the long run, with total real appreciation from 2008 to 2017 of around 19 percent.[11] This compares with a dollar appreciation of 89 percent between 1975 and 1986 (ERS, 2009c). Current world macroeconomic imbalances between the United States and the trade surplus countries of Asia are not corrected.

In the high dollar scenario, the dollar appreciates substantially in real terms from 2008 to 2017 by 39 percent. The macroeconomic imbalances not only persist but become more severe. In the low dollar scenario, the dollar depreciates in the next 3-4 years, more than countering the shortrun appreciation in the second half of 2008, and then more slowly to 2017, with total depreciation from 2008 to 2017 being 4 percent. Continued dollar depreciation in this scenario helps correct global macroeconomic imbalances.

When the dollar exchange rate is changed in the high and low dollar scenarios, the Oxford Model is used to readjust all the other macroeconomic variables affected by the exchange rate, such as GDP growth and inflation for the United States and other countries. The set of macro assumptions entered into PEATSim in each of the dollar scenarios therefore is based on and consistent with the specific values of the dollar exchange rate used in that scenario.

U.S. Agricultural Exports and Trade Prices

Short Run

In the reference scenario in the short run, U.S. agricultural exports fall in value in nominal terms by 18 percent, from $117 billion in 2008 to $96 billion in 2009 (figure 4). However, the drop in real terms (2000 constant prices) is lower at 7 percent. U.S. agricultural exports fall because of decreasing world demand. This is the result of both negative world GDP growth and declining price competitiveness on world markets because of the appreciation of the dollar.

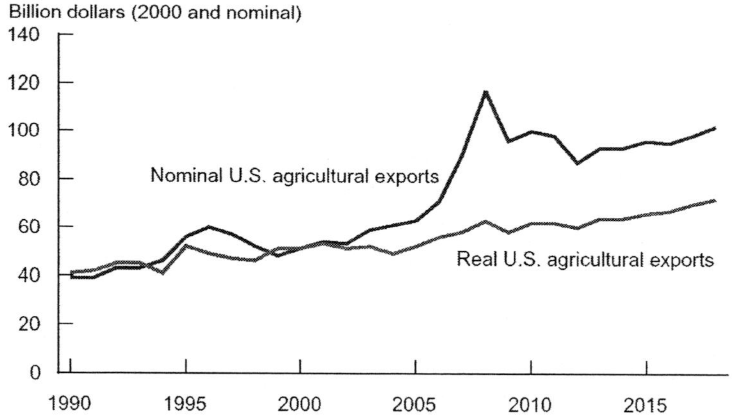

Source: USDA, Economic Research Service (ERS) using USDA's Foreign Agricultural Trade of the United States database; ERS projections.

Figure 4. U.S. agricultural exports and projections *Nominal exports decline while real exports increase after the crisis*

By 2011, however, export prospects improve. Table 1 provides export projections for four major crops and three meats. In the reference scenario, the projected export volume is higher for four of the identified commodities in 2011 than in 2008. Only soybeans show 2011 exports projected substantially below those of 2008. Table 1 also provides projections for the high and low dollar scenarios. The high dollar scenario predictably shows lower exports, and the low dollar scenario shows higher exports. For the crops, the deviations from the reference scenario volumes are not more than 5 percent in any case. For pork and poultry (though not for beef and veal), deviations in the high and low dollar scenarios are much greater.

Table 1. U.S. Exports to the World by Commodity Group by Selected Years

Commodity groupings	Reference scenario, *millions of metric tons*				High dollar scenario, *% deviation from reference*			Low dollar scenario, *% deviation from reference*		
	2008	2011	2013	2017	2011	2013	2017	2011	2013	2017
Wheat	25.9	26.4	26.5	26.6	-0.9	-2.9	-5.1	4.2	1.8	1.1
Rice	3.1	3.7	3.9	4.3	-3.0	-3.8	-11.5	2.7	6.7	6.6
Corn	54.6	58.4	58.5	65.0	-0.1	-0.1	-13.0	2.7	2.5	1.4
Soybeans	24.6	19.7	19.6	18.9	-4.3	-6.4	-8.0	4.7	9.1	17.6
Beef and veal	0.8	0.9	1.0	1.2	-1.7	-0.9	-5.5	1.5	4.5	4.9
Pork	1.4	1.2	1.3	2.0	-23.2	-35.7	-76.4	31.7	70.7	57.3
Poultry	2.9	2.5	2.6	3.0	-11.9	-19.3	-63.6	12.4	32.5	37.9

Source: USDA, Economic Research Service, PEATSim results.

These results demonstrate that world demand for U.S. exports of meat are much more sensitive to changes in the dollar's value than is world demand for U.S. crop exports (or more generally, they show that world demand for meat is more price elastic than demand for crops).

Figure 5 provides the reference scenario projections for U.S. agricultural export prices (or more specifically, U.S. export unit values, which are export values divided by export volumes.) From 2009 to 2012, export prices fall to a nontrivial degree. The export price decline again reflects the crisis-induced fall in world demand for U.S. agricultural exports in the short run. Table 2 provides commodity-specific evidence of the price drop, as prices in 2011 for most of the commodities in the reference scenario are below those in 2008. The table also reveals the degree of sensitivity of world prices to different values for the dollar exchange rate. In the high dollar scenario, world prices are about 5-6 percent lower than in the reference case, while in the low dollar scenario, they are about 5-6 percent higher.

Long Run

Projected U.S. agricultural exports in the long run rise in both the reference and low dollar scenarios to $98 billion and $137 billion in 2017, respectively (figure 6). In the high dollar scenario, exports decline to $68 billion in 2017. The divergence between the high and low scenario projections again reveals the sensitivity of U.S. agricultural exports to the dollar exchange rate. As shown earlier in table 1, similar to the short run, pork and poultry exports (though excluding beef and veal) are much more responsive to exchange rate changes than crop exports.

In the long run, U.S. agricultural export unit values (the proxy for prices) continue to fall but at a lower rate than over 2009-12 (see figure 5). By 2017, in both the high and low dollar scenarios, projected world prices for all commodities deviate from the scenario projections by 16-20 percent—in the high dollar case downward, and in the low dollar case upward (table 2).

Changes in the U.S. dollar exchange rate generally affect meat exports more than crop exports. Yet, crops can still be strongly impacted in the long run. For example, both the U.S. soybean export volume and real price drop significantly in 2009 (figures 7 and 8). After 2009 in the low dollar scenario, the soybean export volume rises through the projection period, while the real price increases and then decreases slightly. However, in the reference scenario, both the export volume and price fall continuously, and in the high dollar scenario, they fall substantially. By 2017, the projected soybean export volume and real price in the low dollar scenario is 28 and 48 percent higher, respectively, than those in the high dollar scenario.

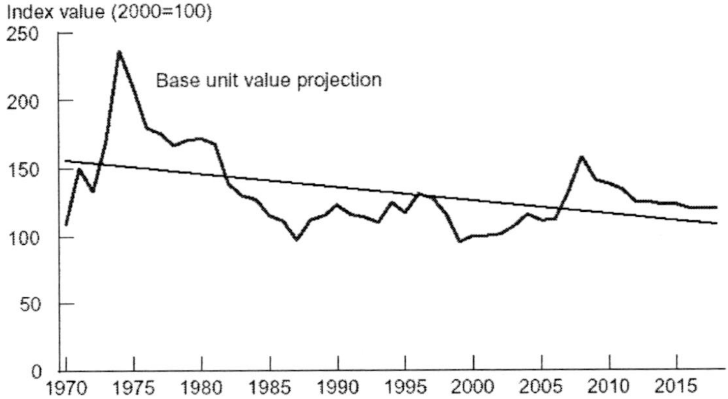

Source: USDA, Economic Research Service using United Nations Food and Agriculture Organization, Agrastat database and U.S. Bureau of Labor Statistics, *BEA End Use Export Indexes, Agricultural Foods, Feeds and Beverages, Excluding Distilled Beverages*; ERS projections.

Figure 5. Real U.S. agricultural export unit value *Agricultural prices move back toward trend values*

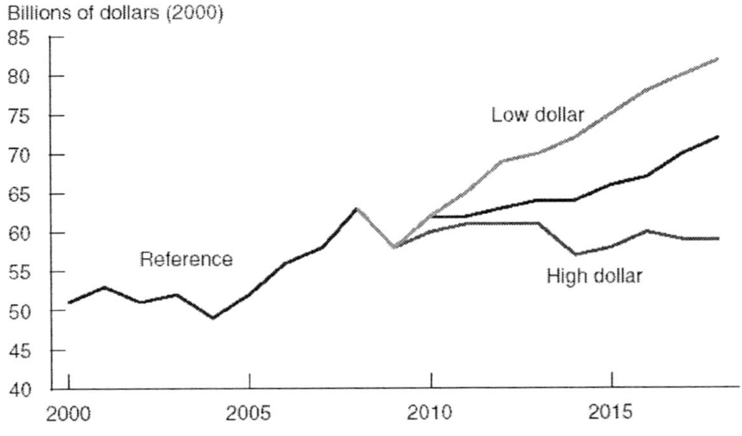

Source: USDA, Economic Research Service (ERS) using USDA's Foreign Agricultural Trade of the United States database and United Nations Food and Agriculture Organization, Agrastat database; ERS projections.

Figure 6. Real agricultural exports and scenario projections *Exchange rate effects can be substantial*

Table 2. Projections for Trade Prices under Alternative Exchange Rates

Commodity groupings	Reference scenario, *dollars per metric ton*				High dollar scenario, *% deviation from reference*			Low dollar scenario, *% deviation from reference*		
	2008	**2011**	**2013**	**2017**	**2011**	**2013**	**2017**	**2011**	**2013**	**2017**
Wheat	214	156	146	142	-5.8	-5.1	-18.8	5.9	17	19.2
Rice	281	281	276	287	-6.2	-5.4	-19.6	5.4	16.5	18.2
Corn	155	127	118	114	-5.8	-3.3	-18.4	5.4	17.3	18.9
Soybeans	363	305	282	269	-6.1	-4.9	-16.9	6.1	17.1	21.4
Beef and veal	892	764	699	638	-5.5	-5.1	-19.3	5.4	15.4	19.4
Pork	1,226	1,253	1,170	1,090	-4.7	-4.7	-17.5	5.1	14.1	16.0
Poultry	1,316	1,214	1,124	1,063	-5.2	-3.9	-17.3	4.8	14.6	17.1

Note: 2008 prices are actual.

Source: USDA, Economic Research Service, PEATSim results.

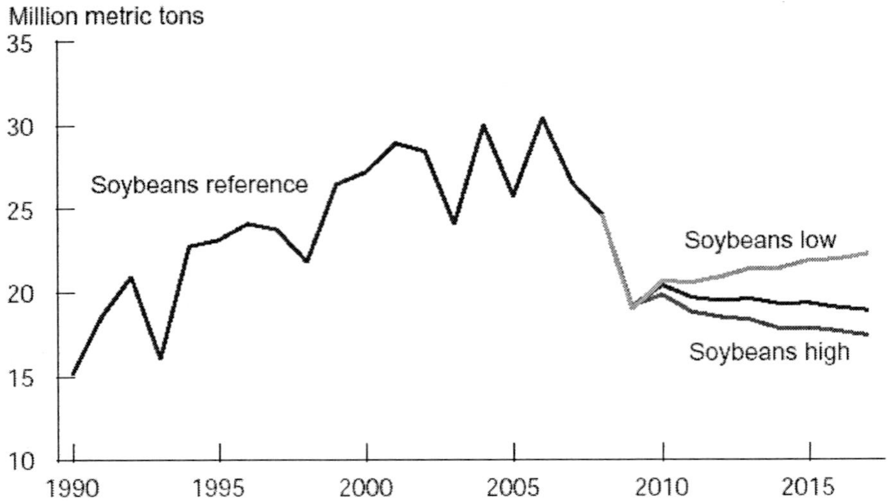

Source: USDA, Economic Research Service, Agricultural Baseline Database and PEATSim simulations.

Figure 7. Real soybean exports under alternative scenario *Soybean exports have come under increasing competitive*

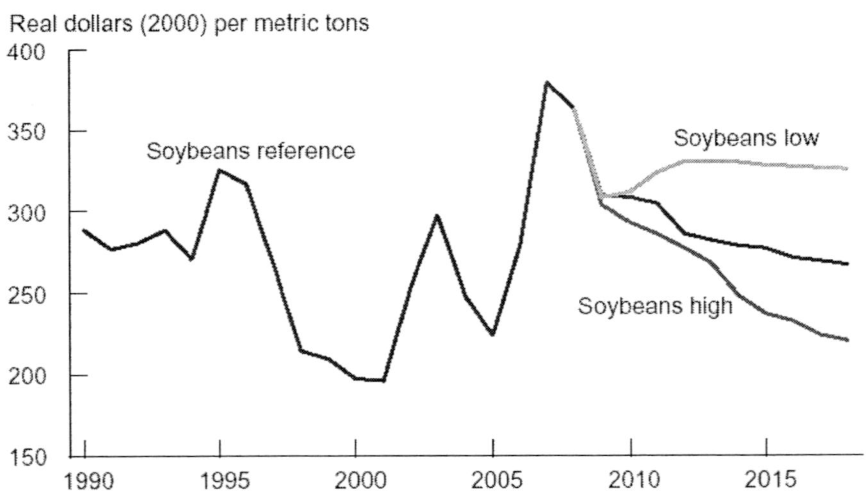

Source: USDA, Economic Research Service, Agricultural Baseline Database and PEATSim simulations.

Figure 8. The real soybean price under alternative scenarios *The soybean price is hit hard by the crisis*

Farm Income

Short Run

The economic crisis puts downward pressure on farm income in the short run. In the reference scenario,[12] net farm income is projected to fall from $89 billion in 2008 to $71 billion in 2009, a drop of 20 percent (figure 9). This decline is from record-high income, so the level in 2009 is still $6 billion above the average annual farm income over 1999-2008 of $65 billion. Net cash farm income[13] is projected to decline from 2008 to 2009 by 17 percent to $77 billion (figure 10).

In the high dollar scenario, lower exports cause farm income to fall because receipts decline faster than expenses. Total expenses are forecast to be slightly higher than the reference case, with greater reductions in fuel and interest expenses being offset by higher feed costs. Because of lower receipts, net farm income in 2009 declines to $60 billion. This is a drop of about a third from 2008 and $11 billion below the reference case. Net cash farm income decreases to $64 billion in the same period.

The livestock sector suffers the most, with receipts projected to be almost 8 percent below the 2009 reference projection of $135 billion, and crop receipts about 1 percent under the 2009 reference projection of $162 billion. Milk and dairy cattle account for most of the decline in livestock receipts—which for dairy producers involves additional contraction beyond an already bleak 2009 outlook in the reference case. A more severe downturn in the U.S. and world economy than was projected in USDA (2009) is expected to further dampen U.S. milk and dairy product sales and dairy exports, driving down dairy product and milk prices to levels not reached since 2000-03.

In the low dollar scenario, net farm income decreases from 2008 to 2009 by 26 percent to $66 billion, and net cash farm income declines to $71 billion.

The dollar is weaker, interest rates higher, and foreign inputs, such as fertilizers, more expensive. Compared with the 2009 scenario results, commodity receipts change very little, and expenses are more than 2 percent higher.

Tighter cash margins over the course of the U.S. and world recession will impact debt repayment ability for some farmers. The most severe effects are expected for dairy farms for which relatively large reductions in cash earnings are projected. In 2007, 5 percent of dairy farms had debt repayments problems, and in the reference scenario, that figure could more than double to 13 percent. In the high dollar scenario, repayment problems could jump to more than one in five for dairy farm businesses.

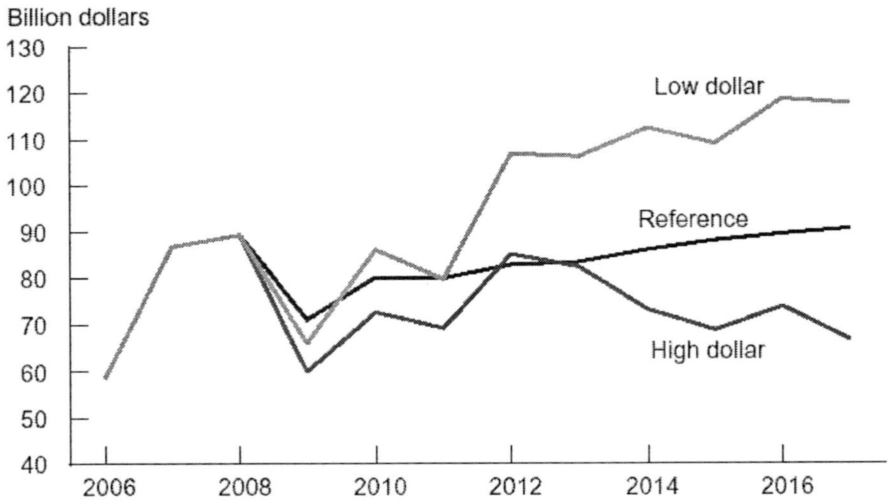

Source: USDA, Economic Research Service.

Figure 9. Net farm income *Exchange rate scenarios make a difference to farm income*

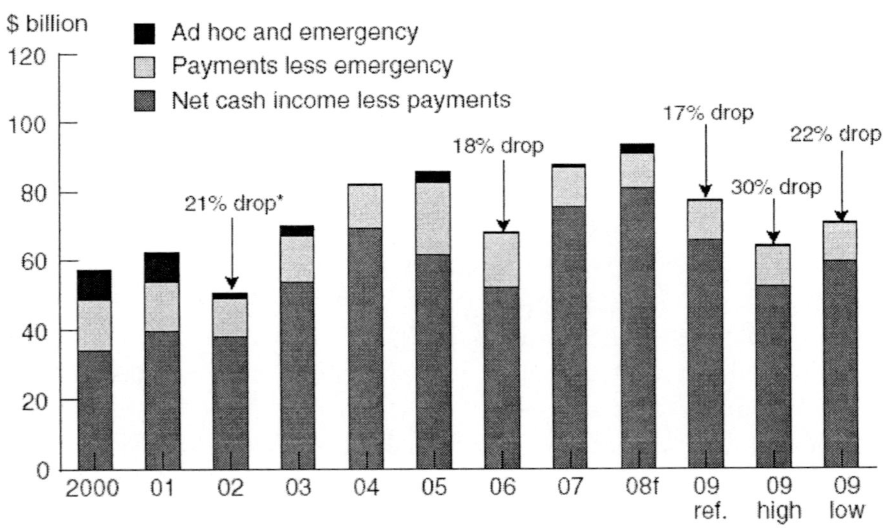

*The percentage change from the prior year. f = forecast.
Source: USDA, Economic Research Service.

Figure 10. Net cash income and farm *payments Exchange rate scenarios make a difference to farm income*

Farm Household Income

Farm household income comes from two sources—income earned specifically from farming and that obtained from off-farm activities and sources. ERS projects that average farm operator household income in 2009 will be $85,140, down from both the 2007 estimate of $86,223 and the 2008 preliminary estimate of $86,864. In real dollars, this becomes $74,107, $81,207, and $78,438, respectively (figure 11). Yet, in every year since 1996, average farm household income has exceeded average U.S. household income. In 2007, for example, the difference was 27 percent. Farm household income is higher than the national household average even if income from farming is excluded. For farm operator households, average income exceeds median income because of the large share of high-income households in the population. In 2007, average (mean) income was $86,223, compared with a median of $52,455.

Over 2003-08, the average annual share of farm earnings in farm household income was only about 12 percent (though it fluctuated from a high of over 17 percent in 2005 to 7.5 percent in 2008). The share could fall in 2009 to 5 percent, as ERS forecasts that average household earnings from farming will drop to $4,144. Although the contribution of farm earnings to farm household income is small, its volatility makes income for farm households more unstable than for households in general.

During the economic crisis, the off-farm income earned by farm households will be more stable than farming income. In 2007, about three-fifths of off-farm income came from wages and salaries earned by farm operators and their spouses.[14] Of the major sectors in which farm operators and their spouses are employed, the two that will probably be the most adversely affected by the economic crisis are manufacturing and construction (figure 12). In 2007, these activities generated 29 percent of wage and salary income for farm operators, though only 11 percent for their spouses. Employment in retail, other private sector services, health, education, and other government services will be more stable during the crisis than work in manufacturing and construction. In 2007, these activities produced 39 percent of wage and salary income for farm operators and 71 percent for spouses. Thirteen percent of off-farm income in 2007 came from steady pensions and government transfer payments (such as social security). The average income of farm households, the dominance of off-farm income in their total income, and the relative stability of employment in the activities that earn most of the off-farm income will all help buffer farm households from the shocks of the economic crisis.

The sources of farm household income, and the share of off-farm earnings in that income, vary considerably by size of farm. ERS does not forecast farm household income by farm size. Yet, the latest estimates (for 2007) show that household income sources differ significantly depending on the size of farms (figure 13).

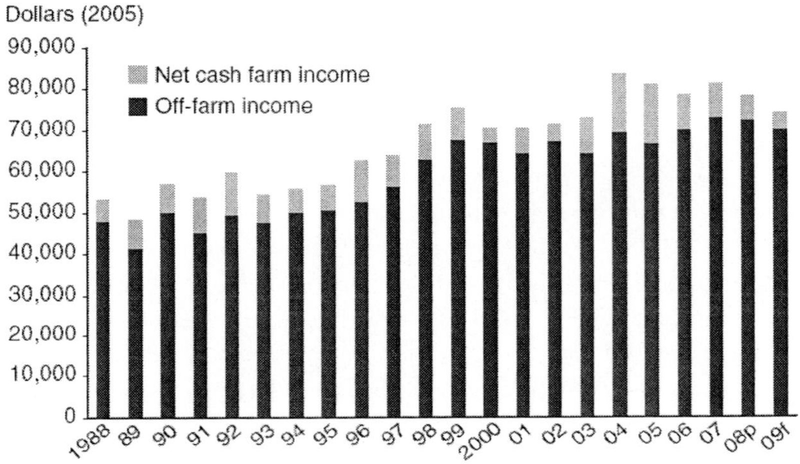

p = preliminary. f = forecast.

Source: USDA, Economic Research Service using USDA's Agricultural Resource Management Survey and U.S. Bureau of the Census, Current Population Survey.

Figure 11. Average real farm operator household income, by source

The large majority of U.S. farms are small, and more than 20 percent have no marketable agricultural production (and thereby earnings) in any given year. On the other hand, in 2007, 5.7 percent of farms accounted for three-quarters of total farm sales. Also in 2007, 92 percent of farm households had farm sales under $250,000. These households had average total income below $80,000 and earned little income from their farms. The other 8 percent of farm households in 2007 (with farm sales above $250,000) had average household income of nearly $180,000, with the bulk from farm earnings. Although the majority of farms are small and generate little income, they hold significant net worth in their land and other farm assets. Their owners' future economic welfare depends not on farm earnings but on farmland values (see box, "Crisis Impacts of U.S. Farm Land Values"). The economic crisis could also affect U.S. agricultural commodity program costs in the short run (see box, "Crisis Impact of U.S. Commodity Program Costs").

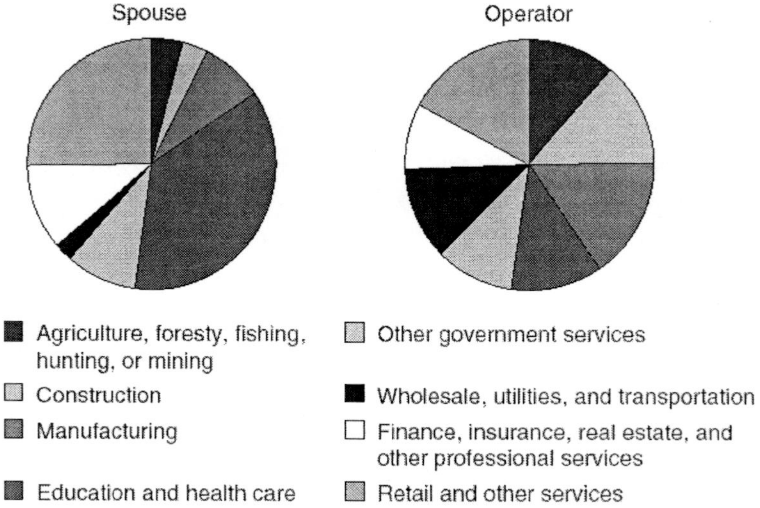

Source: USDA, Economic Research Service using USDA's Agricultural Resource Management Survey.

Figure 12. Industry of wage and salary jobs, operator and spouse, 2007

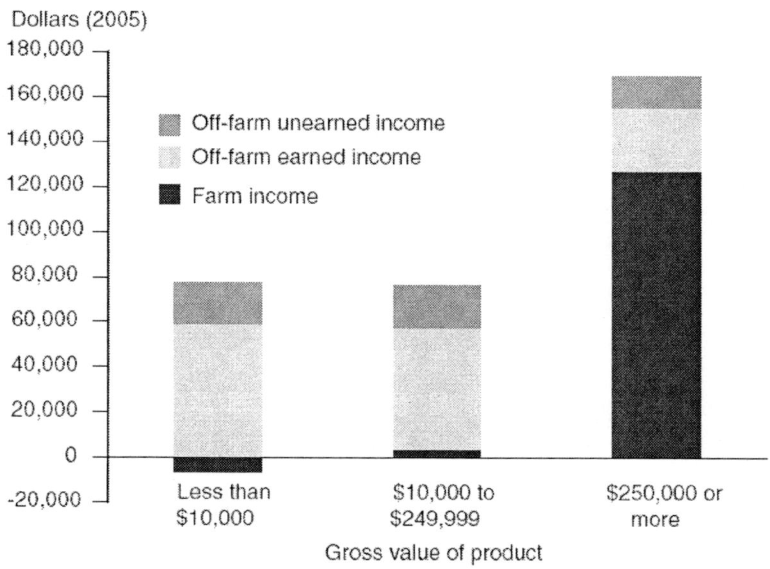

Source: USDA, Economic Research Service using USDA's Agricultural Resource Management Survey.

Figure 13. Real farm operator household income, by size of farm, 2007

Long Run

Farm income is expected to begin to recover in 2010. Yet, the projected strength of the recovery varies considerably across the three exchange rate scenarios. In the reference scenario, net farm income increases by 11 percent to reach $80 billion. The high dollar scenario has a larger relative increase (22 percent) but starts from a much lower 2009 projection and only reaches $73 billion. In the low dollar scenario, net farm income exceeds the reference case in 2010 by $6 billion, hitting $85 billion.

Macroeconomic conditions have a significant impact on projected farm income growth after 2012 (see figure 9). A return to high world income growth expands U.S. agricultural exports, and in the low dollar scenario, exports receive the further boost of enhanced price competitiveness on world markets. Projected farm income rises to $90 billion by 2017 in the reference scenario and to a substantial $118 billion in the low dollar scenario. In the high dollar scenario, exports become less price competitive, and projected 2017 farm income falls to $67 billion. This scenario, in particular, demonstrates how important the exchange rate and exports are to farmers' bottom lines.

ERS does not project farm household income beyond one year into the future (in this case 2009). The bulk of farm household income earned off-farm (from operators and spouses combined) comes from nontrade-dependent activities (construction, retail, wholesale, health, education, and other private and public services). Consequently, the longrun future path of the dollar exchange rate will affect off-farm income much less than farm income. A post-crisis return of the U.S. GDP growth rate to pre-crisis levels therefore should also largely restore off-farm income to pre-crisis levels, regardless of what happens to the exchange rate.

Agricultural Employment

The economic crisis is affecting U.S. employment in the short run, and projected 2009 agricultural export-related employment is expected to fall by 13 percent (a loss of 45,000 jobs) (Edmondson, 2008a). In the longrun reference scenario, projected employment drops by 51,000 jobs over 2008- 17. The employment effects in the high and low dollar scenarios are understandably larger. In the high dollar scenario, agriculture loses 110,000 jobs over 2008-17, compared to a loss of 13,000 jobs by 2017 in the low dollar scenario. The U.S. economy supported almost 116 million jobs in August 2008, and by February 2009 lost more than 4 million, leading to a current unemployment rate of 8.1 percent. Although the changes in agricultural export-related employment are small in number relative to those of the entire

U.S. economy, the job (and corresponding income) shifts would be substantial for agriculture and rural America.

CRISIS'S IMPACT ON U.S. FARMLAND VALUES

The economic crisis will also impact farmland values. Although factors unrelated to agricultural returns affect farmland values to some degree, farm profitability, interest rates, and the inflation rate have had much stronger influence in recent years. At the national level, farm real estate values are projected to fall in 2009 by about 2 percent in the reference case.

Beginning in 2008, certain areas of the United States experienced greater relative adjustment in land values. In several Northeastern States, where nonagricultural factors influence farm real estate more heavily than in other States, farm real estate values have dropped by 2 to 5 percent. In other States, such as California, Florida, and Nevada, which have been experiencing a contraction in the rural housing market, there has been no growth, or even a drop, in values. States where corn and soybeans constitute a major share of agricultural production have seen double-digit increases in land values because of the biofuels expansion. In the high dollar scenario, where prices and receipts for corn and soybeans fall below those in the reference case, land values in such States as Illinois, Indiana, and Minnesota are expected to moderate in 2009. Farmland in these areas is still viewed as a viable counterinflationary investment, and any downward pressure could be buoyed by demand from large pension funds and institutional investors.

Farm real estate values are not very sensitive to short-term changes in the returns to agriculture. The main reason is that, as with any asset, the value of farmland should equal the discounted value of the expected future streams of income earned from owning the asset. The major factor that drives changes in farm real estate values is the underlying long-term expectation of returns. Since this changes only slowly, farmland values tend to be relatively stable compared with other aspects of U.S. agriculture. Even so, over the projection period, the annual growth rate in farmland values returns to 5 percent in nominal terms and 3 percent in real terms. This is a big shift from the 12-percent annual growth rate in the value of U.S. farm real estate during 2004-08, adjusted for inflation.

Concerning the long-term impact of the crisis on farm real estate values, there is a substantial difference in value at the end of the projection period between the high and low dollar scenarios. Farm real estate values in the high dollar scenario are projected to be $264 billion less than those of the low dollar scenario by 2017.

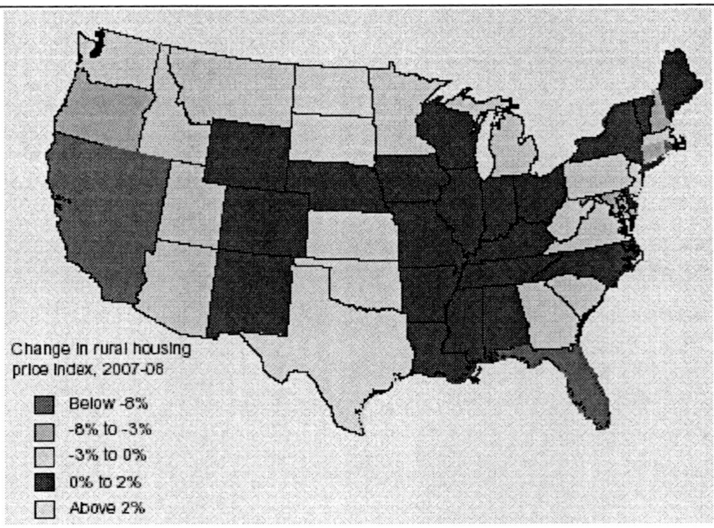

Source: USDA, Economic Research Service using data from Office of Federal Housing Enterprise Oversight.

Changes in rural housing prices by State

Crisis's Impact on U.S. Commodity Program Costs

The 2008 Farm Act provides three price-dependent programs—marketing loans, counter-cyclical payments (CCP), and average crop revenue election (ACRE) payments—for program crops. (The program crops include wheat, feed grains, soybeans, minor oilseeds, rice, upland cotton, peanuts, and pulse crops.) The table provides USDA Baseline projected market prices and commodity program price triggers for five major program crops. With the exception of prices for upland cotton, prices in crop years 2009/10 and 2010/11 should remain well above marketing loan rates and CCP effective target prices, indicating that program costs for the marketing loan and CCP programs would be minimal. Program costs are likely to be incurred for upland cotton, with prices projected near the marketing loan rate and well below the CCP effective target price. Any price reductions due to the crisis, particularly in the high dollar scenario, would raise these program costs. Cotton program costs averaged almost $2 billion per year in 2002-07.

The impact of the financial crisis on participation in the ACRE program and costs for the program is less clear. Producers can elect to participate in ACRE beginning in 2009. Once they elect ACRE, they must remain in the program through the 2012 crop year. They also must give up 20 percent of their direct payments and have their marketing loan rates cut by 30 percent. If it is assumed that yields per planted acre are similar to the 5-year Olympic average (the yearly average after dropping both the highest and lowest year values) used for ACRE, then ACRE payments would be based on price movements. Using the price projections in the table, comparison of 90 percent of the 2-year average price used for ACRE suggests that this program would be an attractive option for producers of wheat, rice and soybeans. If producers elect ACRE, the 20-percent reduction in direct payments will be partially offset by ACRE payments. Once again, any crisis-related price reductions would raise potential costs of this program. However, any fall in commodity prices in a year would reduce the 2 year average price used to determine ACRE payments in subsequent years, thereby lowering payments.

Commodity program crop price triggers

Item	Years	Wheat	Corn	Rice	Soybeans	Upland cotton
	*Dollars**					
Price	2009/10	5.75	4.00	12.50	8.85	0.5000
	2010/11	5.60	3.90	11.45	8.75	0.5500
Marketing loan rate	2009/10	2.75	1.95	6.50	5.00	0.5200
Counter-cyclical payment effective target price	2009/10	3.40	2.35	8.15	5.36	0.6458
90 percent of ACRE 2-year average price	2009/10	5.98	3.65	13.19	8.71	0.4950
	2010/11	5.65	3.56	13.05	7.77	0.4500

*Dollars per bushel (wheat, corn, and soybeans) per hundredweight (rice), and per pound (cotton).

Note: Assumes USDA price projections. Lower prices in 2009/10 would reduce the effective ACRE price guarantee.

Source: USDA, Economic Research Service.

RESILIENCY OF U.S. AGRICULTURE

There are a number of reasons why U.S. agriculture may be in a relatively strong position to withstand the temporary shocks that will result from the current financial uncertainty and unfavorable economic climate. In addition to greater involvement in world markets, other important differences exist between today's agriculture and the sector that endured its last major financial crisis more than 20 years ago. Farmers now have a wider range of risk management tools, such as leasing, contracting, renting, crop insurance, hedging, and direct government payments, to share market and financial risks. Farmers today produce higher valued products as a result of technological improvements in agricultural production and food processing systems, as well as have better information on changing consumer preferences. Technological advances have also spurred productivity growth through higher yields. Farmers have improved control over their operations, spend more on management services, and increasingly adopt cost-saving technologies such as hybrid seed, water-saving irrigation platforms, and electronic yield-monitoring devices.

Farmers emerged from the last credit crisis in agriculture more conservative in their use of debt financing. Many more farmers now pay cash for land, equipment, and inputs. Farmers are also reducing their debt load by leasing assets such as land and machinery. Farm lending has shifted from being based mainly on collateral to giving more consideration to borrowers' ability to service debt. Farm sector debt-to-equity is projected to be below 10 percent in 2009 and has not exceeded 20 percent since the late 1980s. It would take a 40-percent reduction in asset values to reach 20 percent debt-to equity, or a combination of a 30-percent increase in debt and a 30-percent reduction in asset values. The largest annual reduction in farm real estate values since 1970 was 12 percent in 1984. The largest annual increase in debt was 19 percent in 1979.

CONCLUSION

The emerging global economic crisis has major impacts on U.S. agriculture. As the global recession takes hold, global income falls and demand for agricultural imports from countries around the world declines. That drop in global income combined with the shortrun appreciation of the dollar will lead to substantially lower U.S. agricultural exports in the short to medium term. These developments in turn will reduce agricultural commodity prices, lower farm income and employment, and put downward pressure on agricultural real estate values. Agricultural households will suffer from declining income from off-farm jobs, as the economic recession in the United States ripples through to rural-based businesses and loss of tax revenue puts pressure on rural government employment and social services.

On the positive side for U.S. agriculture, the sector went into the crisis with record-high exports, prices, and income. Consequently, the effects of the crisis will be less severely felt by agriculture than by many other sectors of the U.S. economy.

The main long-term issue is how and whether the fundamental imbalances that created the conditions for the global crisis will be reduced or maintained. This process will depend to a large degree on whether exchange rates are realigned. If, in the longer term, the dollar and other trade deficit countries' currencies depreciate, then imbalances will be reduced and economic growth will resume at sustainable rates. If exchange rates are not realigned, then the trade and savings imbalances will remain.

This study's high and low dollar scenarios represent the resolution of these imbalances and to a large degree depend on how exchange rates are realigned. The consequences for U.S. agriculture of this long-term outcome are profound. If the long-term outcome is a depreciated dollar and the fundamental realignment of global exchange rates, then U.S. agriculture will be strengthened by increases in agricultural export volumes, agricultural commodity prices, and farm incomes. If the long-term outcome is an appreciation of the dollar but no fundamental realignment of exchange rates, the high dollar will become a constraint on U.S. agricultural exports, dollar-denominated agricultural commodity prices, and farm incomes.

In the long run, sustainable world growth depends on getting the balance right between economic growth, agricultural output, and resource availability. That balance depends on technological advances that result in discovery of new and alternative energy sources, efficiency gains in the production and use of energy, agricultural science (such as genetic engineering), and other primary resources. Given agriculture's control of a major part of U.S. land resources, much of the new developments in energy (such as wind turbines and solar technology) will require use of current farmland. Technological breakthroughs, such as horizontal drilling, will also increase oil and natural gas production on agricultural land, thereby raising royalty income paid to farm households. Farmers will continue to be suppliers of feedstocks for biofuels. Technological gains in the use of water, treatment for pests, and other technologies will positively affect yields. Efficiency gains in the production and use of energy will also have major impacts on agricultural production, since energy-related inputs are the largest single cost to farmers.

To the degree that the current crisis results in a rebalancing that supports the development of new agricultural and energy technologies, the longer term outlook is that U.S. agriculture will continue to be a major participant in the changing structure of the economy. In such a world, agriculture would continue to provide a plentiful supply of food at reasonable prices.

REFERENCES

Board of Governors of the Federal Reserve System (2009). *Flow of Funds Accounts.*

Edmondson, William (2008a). *U.S. Agricultural Trade Boosts Overall Economy*, E-Outlook Report FAU-124, U.S. Department of Agriculture, Economic Research Service, *www.ers.usda.gov/publications/ fau/2008/ 04apr/ fau124/*

Edmondson, William (2008b). "*Agricultural Trade Multipliers: Effects of Trade on the U.S. Economy*," U.S. Department of Agriculture, Economic Research Service, www.ers.usda.gov/data/ trademultiplier/ econeffects/ 2007 overview.aspx

Executive Office of the President, Council of Economic Advisors (2009). "Housing and Financial Markets," in *Economic Report of the Council of Economic Advisors,* pp. 61-96.

Food and Agriculture Organization of the United Nations (FAO) (2009). "Agrastat."

Federal Deposit Insurance Corporation (FDIC) (2008). *FDIC Quarterly*, 2(4), http://www.fdic.gov/bank/analytical/quarterly/2008_vol2_4/ FDIC 1 39_QuarterlyVol2No4_Web.pdf

Global Insight (2009). *Interim Forecast Spreadsheet (February)*, Cambridge, MA.

Krugman, Paul (2008). *The International Finance Multiplier*, unpublished paper.

Lewis, Michael (2008). "*The End of the Wall Street Boom*," Conde Nast Portfolio.com, December.

Liefert, William, and Mathew Shane (2000). "The Macroeconomic Linkages to Agriculture," in *International Financial Crisis and Agriculture*, International Agriculture and Trade Report WRS-93-3, pp. 8-14, U.S. Department of Agriculture, Economic Research Service.

Shane, Mathew, and David Stallings (1987). *The World Debt Crisis and Its Resolution,* Foreign Agricultural Economic Report 231, U.S. Department of Agriculture, Economic Research Service.

Shane, Mathew, Terry Roe, & Agapi Somwaru (2008). "Exchange Rates,

Foreign Income, and U.S. Agricultural Exports," *Agricultural and Resource Economics Review, 37*(2), 160-175.

Trostle, Ronald (2008). *Global Agricultural Supply and Demand: Factors Contributing to the Recent Increase in Food Commodity Prices*, Outlook Report WRS-0801, U.S. Department of Agriculture, Economic Research Service, www.ers.usda.gov/publications/wrs0801/

U.S. Bureau of Labor Statistics (2009). *BEA End Use Export Indexes, Agricultural Foods, Feeds and Beverages, Excluding Distilled Beverages*, www.bls.gov/web

U.S. Department of Agriculture. "Foreign Agricultural Trade of the United States," www.ers.usda.gov/data/fatus/

U.S. Department of Agriculture, Economic Research Service (ERS) (2009a). "*Bioenergy Briefing Room*," www.ers.usda.gov/briefing/bioenergy

U.S. Department of Agriculture, Economic Research Service (ERS) (2009b). "*Farm Income and Costs Briefing Room*," *www.ers.usda. gov/ briefing/farmincome/*

U.S. Department of Agriculture, Economic Research Service (ERS) (2009c). "Ag Exchange Rate Data Set," www.ers.usda.gov/ data/ exchangerates/

U.S. Department of Agriculture, Economic Research Service (ERS) (2009d). "*International Macroeconomic Data Set*,"www.ers.usda.gov/ data/ macroeconomics

U.S. Department of Agriculture, Economic Research Service (ERS) (2009e). "*Farm Household Economics and Well-Being Briefing Room: Beginning Farmers, Demographics, and Labor Allocations*," www.ers.usda. gov/briefing/wellbeing/demographics.htm

U.S. Department of Agriculture, Economic Research Service (ERS) (2009f). "*Farm Household Economics and Well-Being Briefing Room: Farm Household Income*," *www.ers.usda.gov/briefing/wellbeing/farmhousein come.htm*

U.S. Department of Agriculture, Economic Research Service (ERS) (2009g). "*Food Assistance and Nutrition Programs Briefing Room*," www.ers.usda.gov/briefing/foodnutritionassistance/

U.S. Department of Agriculture, Office of the Chief Economist (USDA) (2008). *USDA Agricultural Projections to 2017*, Long-term Projections Report OCE-2008-1.

U.S. Department of Agriculture, Office of the Chief Economist (USDA) (2009). *USDA Agricultural Projections to 2018*, Long-term Projections Report OCE-2009-1.

U.S. Department of Commerce, Bureau of the Census (2008). *Current Population Survey.*

U.S. Department of Energy, Energy Information Agency (EIA) (2008). *Inter-national Energy Outlook, 2008*, www.eia.doe. gov/ oiaf/ forecasting

U.S. Department of Energy, Energy Information Agency (EIA) (2009). *Weekly All Countries Spot Price, FOB*, http://tonto.eia.doe. gov/ dnav/ pet/hist/wtotworldw.htm

Wolf, Martin (2008). *Fixing Global Finance*, Baltimore, MD: Johns Hopkins University Press.

World Bank (2008). *World Development Indicators.*

End Notes

[1] Rural housing prices declined more than 8 percent in California, Nevada, Florida, and Rhode Island. They declined between 3 and 8 percent in Oregon, Maryland, New Hampshire, and Connecticut. On the other hand, rural housing prices increased in the Dakotas, Kansas, Oklahoma, Texas, West Virginia, and Delaware. See map on page 24.

[2] There is a lot of uncertainty about exactly how the current recession will play out. While the consensus forecast is for growth to resume by the end of 2009 or early 2010, the severity of recession in most countries has been consistently revised upward during the past year.

[3] A special analysis was conducted to establish the reference scenario used in this report. This scenario was developed in January 2009, based on U.S. and global macroeconomic conditions at that time.

[4] High world growth also put upward pressure on prices for energy and agricultural goods because resource availability could not be increased quickly enough in the short run. This is one reason why world energy and many agricultural commodity prices increased dramatically in 2007-08 (Trostle, 2008).

[5] Bulk commodities are defined as crops such as corn, barley, wheat, soybeans, rice, and raw tobacco where there has been no processing. High- value products include any agricultural product that has undergone some processing. We usually divide high-value products into intermediate products such as soybean meal and oil, produce and horticulture such as fruits and vegetables, and consumer-ready processed products such as confectionary goods and breakfast cereals.

[6] While not usually considered farming, many farm activities involve processing of farm products where the proceeds go to the farmer. Examples of this include dairy farms that make cheese, vineyards that produce and bottle their wine, fruit farmers that box their fruit for shipment to grocery stores, and farms that transport their products to market.

[7] The share of agricultural production that is exported varies by commodity. For example, between 2004 and 2006, the United States exported around 71 percent of cotton, 50 percent of wheat, and 30 percent of rice, but only 3 percent of beef (see the summary chart in Edmondson, 2008b).

[8] The evolving dynamics of the current global crisis are remarkably similar to those of previous crises. Global imbalances result in large capital flows to countries, which lead to risky loans and investment. If capital then quickly flows out of countries, it can cause a financial crisis (Shane and Stallings, 1987; Liefert and Shane, 2000).

[9] Some food spending will be affected by the health of the general economy, which, in turn, affects the use of USDA's food and nutrition assistance programs. Caseloads for the Supplemental Nutrition Assistance Program (SNAP, formerly known as the Food Stamp Program) tend to follow the unemployment rate, a key indicator of the health of the general economy. The relationship is less pronounced for the other food and nutrition assistance programs. In turn, the food assistance programs affect industry and the general economy. Demand for farm and processed food products increases when program spending rises, and SNAP participation grows during economic downturns, which can have a stabilizing effect on the economy (ERS, 2009g).

[10] A depreciation of the dollar also results in rising real U.S. interest rates and the crowding out of domestic investment, as a larger share of domestic saving must finance the U.S. fiscal deficit.

[11] A change in the real, as opposed to nominal, value of the dollar is calculated by adjusting the change in the nominal value by the difference between the inflation (or deflation) rates in the United States and its trading partners.

[12] Note that projected 2009 net farm income and cash income in the reference case are above the levels projected in both the high and low dollar scenarios. The reason is that the reference scenario is based on macroeconomic assumptions (such as GDP growth and exchange rates) made in October 2008, while the high and low dollar scenarios are based on macro variable assumptions made later in January 2009, when the world economic outlook was bleaker.

[13] Net cash income is a measure of cash available to farmers to meet expenditures and service debt. Net farm income reflects only the earnings from production that occurred in the current year.

[14] Three-quarters of off-farm income comes from wages and salaries and off-farm businesses. Retirement and other transfer income makes up about 13 percent of farm household income, with most coming from public sources. Other important sources of income include interest and dividend income. The ERS forecast of 2009 off-farm income is based on the latest available forecasts of 2009 U.S. gross domestic product and labor compensation as of the release date, February 12, 2009 (see www.ers.usda.gov/briefing/wellbeing/ farmhouse income.htm).

Chapter Sources

The following chapters have been previously published:

Chapter 1 – This is an edited, reformatted and augmented version of United States Department of Agriculture publication, Report WRS-09-05 dated August 2009.

Chapter 2 – This is an edited, reformatted and augmented version of United States Department of Agriculture publication, Report WRS-09-02 dated March 2009.

INDEX

A

B

C

T

U

V

W

Y